AF408507

RMF

Security Control Assessor

NIST 800-53A Security Control Assessment Guide

Book 3

NIST 800 Cybersecurity

By

Bruce Brown, CISSP, ISC2 CGRC

Copyright © 2022 by Bruce Brown

All rights reserved. No part of this publication may be reproduced, distributed, or transmitted in any form or by any means, including photocopying, recording, or other electronic or mechanical methods, without the prior written permission of the publisher, except in the case of brief quotations embodied in critical reviews and certain other noncommercial uses permitted by copyright law.

For permission requests, write to the publisher, addressed "Attention: Permissions Coordinator," at the address below.

www.convocourses.com

contact@convocourses.com

Join Convocourses:

Download free templates, sample documents, and videos based on the NIST 800-53 controls.

Use coupon RMFISSOSCA25 to get 25% off your first purchase!

Check us out on:

youtube.com/convocourses

Contact us:

contact@convocourses.com

Table of Contents

About this book

Like all NIST 800 cybersecurity series books, this is not meant to replace the government back resources such as NIST 800-37, NIST 800-53, or NIST 800-53A. This book is a guide to help navigate the security control assessors tasked with NIST 800 systems.

For NIST 800 assessor templates, go to:
www.convocourses.com/assessortemplates

Copyright © 2022 by Bruce Brown

Khobar Towers & And Disaster Prep

A terrorist bomb inflicted maximum damage on a military housing complex in Saudi Arabia in 1996. A truck filled with explosives was parked next to the fence line of Khobar Towers, an eight-story military housing complex. The detonation killed 19 service members and injured over 400 others.

Some of my co-workers were in Khobar Towers when it was hit. One of them was still digging out glass from the side of his face. X-rays cannot detect glass.

As bad as this terrorist attack was, it could have been much worse. Luckily, they'd changed the security tactics based on a vulnerability assessment from another terrorist attack at a base not too far away. A year before the bombing of Khobar Towers, there'd been a car bomb at a base in Riyadh, Saudi Arabia. The assessment of that bombing led to some changes to security practices on the towers. While the fence line had been too close, leadership had decided to post a security unit on the top of the buildings.

That security unit evacuated as many airmen as possible when they saw the truck parking too close to the building. The quick actions of the security forces on the buildings saved many lives.

Copyright © 2022 by Bruce Brown

The Assessments I've Done

I have been doing cyber security compliance since 2000, but I have conducted security assessments since the 90s. My security career started when I got a low score on the Armed Services Aptitude Battery (ASVAB) test, and they stuck me in a job that matched my horrible scores, Security Forces. I wanted to do avionics, electronics, or thermonuclear physics, but instead, they had me protecting the eggheads who had the talent to do them.

I hated being in Security Forces. It was a thankless, brutal job, a wolf pack that ate their own. The regular Air Force looked down on us because they thought we weren't smart enough. When we worked with the Army, they said we had it easy, and the Marines… only made grunting noises, so we could not understand what they were saying.

Security Forces was hard, and I did not like it, but it taught me that no one cares what I like or hate because, in security, there is a job to do, and if someone doesn't do it, people can die. So, the choice is "do you want people to die?" or "do you want to do your damn job?"

Security Forces taught me the fundamentals of security. Identify the asset you need to protect, identify weaknesses that could be exploited by the most likely threats, and conduct assessments to ensure security measures are in place. This applies in all areas of security, whether you are guarding a C-130 aircraft, writing secure code, or protecting a network. Security Forces must conduct assessments often. I had to conduct them myself as a Security Forces leader, but I received the organization's assessments more often.

When I retook the military test and got an acceptable score, I could cross-train into information technology, 3C0X1, computer operator. I was hoping to be a network engineer, but instead, I got

Copyright © 2022 by Bruce Brown

pushed into certification & accreditation, an ancient version of governance, risk, and compliance (GRC).

It was a job no one else wanted to do in a secure facility with no windows. I asked people how to do it, and no one could help me. I read the information security policy, which kept referencing other documents. I read the federal laws that the document let me to. If it pointed to a directive from the Department of Defense, I would read that. If it mentioned other policies and procedures, I would look for those and read them. It was like deciphering a puzzle. After a while, it started to make sense. Fundamentally, it was like the physical security practices that we were taught in Security Forces, only without the weapons, combat, and hostage situation training.

I learned that, just like physical security, assessments were a huge part of security compliance. Self-assessment and third-party assessments were conducted regularly.

Since then, certification and accreditation have been replaced with a process focused on risk management, authorization, and assessments. With the old certification and accreditation process, it seemed like all we did was create a bunch of policy and procedure documents that no one read. These days I'm deep in the weeds on conducting security compliance for the public and private sectors.

As of 2022, the number of terrorist attacks has increased, but the cyber-attack rate is even more alarming. The environment is more hostile than ever, with cyber security attacks happening every few seconds to organizations worldwide.

Security assessments are more important than they ever were.

Copyright © 2022 by Bruce Brown

Assessments of Panama

In 1989, An activist group infiltrated the Pacific Swan, a ship bound for the Panama Canal. The ship was carrying 70 tons of nuclear waste. The ship needed to go from France to Japan through the fragile Panama Canal's man-made locking system, which allowed international goods to go from the Atlantic to the Pacific Ocean.

The activists didn't agree with governments shipping nuclear waste across the sea. I have to say, I agree, but I don't think sneaking aboard a ship and tying yourself to a vessel's mast is going to stop this.

``We are not trying to stop the ship's passage through the canal, but we wanted to show our opposition to nuclear transport using a direct action," said the spokesman of Greenpeace, Carlos Bravo.

As security professionals, we must consider the disastrous implications of this. This could have gone differently. Imagine if a criminal organization, rogue government, or terror cell gained complete control of the world's most strategic waterway. They could place a stranglehold on international commerce. Or maybe just cripple commerce by destroying part of the Locks. Over 13,000 ships per year cross the Panama Canal, which joins the Atlantic and Pacific oceans.

Security concerns existed when the US military surrendered the Panama Canal to the Republic of Panama in 1999. The concerns were justified because the Revolutionary Armed Forces of Columbia (FARC) guerillas regularly staged forays into Panamanian territory. The National Liberation Army in Columbia would try to get attention and money for their cause by hijacking and mass kidnappings. Although these groups didn't have the canal on their minds, it was a

Copyright © 2022 by Bruce Brown

concern because it was a soft target with little protection. All it would take was a little imagination and a well-placed shoulder-fired weapon.

After decades of security assessments from private and public organizations worldwide, the Panama Canal got a major modern upgrade to its security.

In 2004, the Panama Canal implemented enhanced security processes and procedures. They applied the requirements of the International Ship and Port Facility Security (ISPS) Code and received fulfillment certification from the American Bureau of Shipping (ABS) Consulting. The Panama Canal Authority (ACP) pursued the certification. The ACP was among the first maritime organizations in the continent to receive ISPS certification. The ISPS code requires that processes improve the way the Canal works with port facilities and ships to detect and deter security threats within a repeatable standard in a consistent framework. The Panama Canal is required to exchange security information, establish methods to assess security and enforce safety measures.

Every industry with important assets and information must have some sort of assessment process. Organizations that neglect a robust assessment process are eventually taken advantage of by threats that exploit weaknesses. Assessments don't prevent attacks from happening, but they can minimize their impact of them.

Copyright © 2022 by Bruce Brown

What is an Assessment?

A security control assessment tests and evaluates information systems, facilities, and processes security features.

For a deeper understanding of what assessments are, you need to know more about the source of the assessments. The context of the assessment is everything.

Security assessments are based on industry, private and federal standards. Sarbanes-Oxley (SOX) Act of 2002, known as SOX compliance, is a standard in the financial sector that includes monetary transactions and information security audits that banks and other major financial institutions must do. Retail stores with point-of-sale devices that collect your credit card information are subject to the Payment Card Industry Data Security Standard (PCI/DSS) and its assessments. Verizon, IBM, and other private companies offer risk and compliance assessments to small, medium, and large organizations.

Governments also have security standards that must be met. The US is not the only country with a security standard like the NIST 800-37 risk management framework process that includes assessments. Almost every country has its own.

An assessment gives a certain level of confidence that security features are in place and working properly. Each organization has a slightly different implementation of the security control assessment process.

They follow the rules and regulations, and these laws give enough room, so there is no "one size fits all" approach to implementation.

Copyright © 2022 by Bruce Brown

We aim to ensure you know the peaks, valleys, and overall landscape to navigate any organization implementing these federal laws.

This book will focus on the NIST 800's implementation of assessments. The process is described in NIST 800-37, 800-53, 800-53A, and 800-115:

- NIST 800-37, Risk Management Framework for Information Systems and Organizations: A System Life Cycle Approach for Security and Privacy

- NIST 800-53, Security and Privacy Controls for Information Systems and Organizations

- NIST 800-53A, Assessing Security and Privacy Controls in Information Systems and Organizations

- NIST 800-115, Technical Guide to Information Security Testing and Assessment

As with all aspects of security compliance, understanding how NIST 800 controls are assessed will help you understand the process of most security compliance frameworks, whether industry-based, private or government based.

Quick Overview of the NIST 800-37 process

You are expected to understand the NIST 800 process and the controls before you get too deep into how the assessments are done. But here is a quick high-level overview of how the NIST 800-37 RMF works.

The NIST 800 risk management framework consists of a seven-step process. This process aims to reduce the impacts on assets if disaster strikes. Disasters include (but are not limited to) earthquakes, Frank Jonson from accounting accidentally crashing the server, or an attack from a former Soviet Union country hell-bent on establishing relevance.

Copyright © 2022 by Bruce Brown

This process is done for each major system within an "authorization boundary." Authorization boundary is a fancy term that means the same boss controls networked systems. Each major group of networked systems goes through the NIST 800-37 process:

1. Prepare – coordinate with stakeholders and gather data to start the process for the system.

2. Categorize – Determine the security categorization of the group of systems. Categories are Low, Moderate, or High.

3. Select – Determine which controls will be used based on the category and the systems.

4. Implement – install, configure, or put security control to protect the system.

5. Assess – Analyze to determine if the security controls have been implemented effectively.

6. Authorize – Upper-level management accepts the remaining risks of the system in writing.

7. Monitor – Continuously observe any changes to the system, threats, or environment.

Copyright © 2022 by Bruce Brown

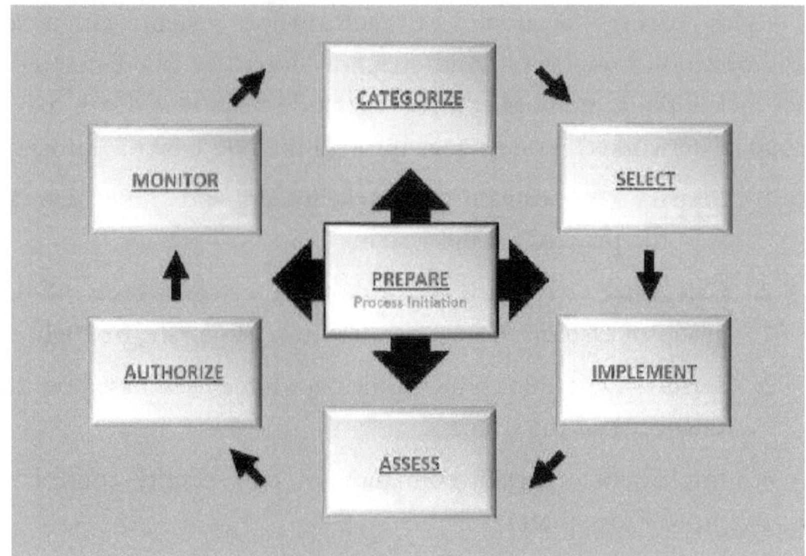

NIST SP 800-37, Steps

For more on this process, see Book 1, RMF ISSO: Foundations. See Book 2, RMF ISSO: NIST 800 Controls, for more on the controls.

Copyright © 2022 by Bruce Brown

Security Control Assessor

The Cybersecurity & Infrastructure Security Agency (CISA) describes the security controls assessor as someone who "This role conducts independent, comprehensive assessments of the management, operational, and technical security controls and control enhancements employed within or inherited by an information technology (IT) system to determine the overall effectiveness of the controls (as defined in NIST SP 800-37)."

In other words, a security control assessor analyzes how well the security features have been implemented on an organization's computers, networks, and processes.

I have heard the role called an assessor, a validator, certifying authority, an Information assurance compliance analyst and auditor, and (my favorite) an SCA.

Some federal agencies have started using the term SCA-V or SCA-O. For SCA-V, the "V" is for the validator. These roles perform risk assessment so that a system can obtain (or renew) authorization to operate. SCA-O sometimes refers to the "organization" tasked with conducting the assessment.

Each organization has its name for the same type of work, so we won't entertain every type in each industry. We will focus on what you need to know. Many of the definitions, names, and acronyms change like the wind.

What doesn't change much is the types of knowledge, skill, and tasks expected of an assessor.

Copyright © 2022 by Bruce Brown

SCA Core knowledge

There are certain things that the assessor needs to understand before they start. The National Initiative for Cybersecurity Education (NICE) Cybersecurity Workforce lists specific core knowledge for SCA work:

- Computer network concepts, protocols, and network security methods

- Risk management process

- Laws, regulations, policies, and ethics related to cybersecurity.

- Cybersecurity privacy principles (security best practices)

- Cyber threats and vulnerabilities

- Organization's evaluation and validation

- Security assessment process

- Information technology security principles (firewall, DMZ, encryption)

- Penetration testing principles, tools, and techniques

If you are doing security control assessments for information systems and the infrastructure that supports them, some understanding is required in these core areas. The level of knowledge depends on what the assessor's tasks include. Some assessments may require someone who is a subject matter expert to consult, represent or be a part of the assessment to ensure the correct knowledge level is at the disposal of the assessor.

SCA Core Skill & Abilities

Skills and abilities are heavily dependent on the scope of the assessment. For example, if the assessment requires a penetration test, the assessor will need a strong skillset in things like fingerprinting an operating system, port scanning, enumeration, and some applicable tools. At the same time, a policy and procedure assessment might

Copyright © 2022 by Bruce Brown

require skills and ability in NIST risk management framework compliance.

Core skills and abilities include:

- Skills in determining how a security system should work.
- Skills in discerning the protection needs (security controls on a system)

Additional skills and abilities include, but are not limited to:

- Skills doing vulnerability scans
- Skills protecting confidentiality, integrity, and availability
- Skills interfacing with customers
- Skills in preparing the test & evaluation reports
- Ability to identify systematic security issues based on analysis of vulnerabilities
- Ability to ask clarifying questions
- Ability to communicate effectively

The site NICCS.CISA.GOV lists many other skills, abilities, and knowledge, but honestly, these depend on the scope of what needs to be done. When the scope of the assessment is a general support system with multiple physical locations, different operating systems, network devices, and processes, then there is a need for an assessment team.

Tasks of the SCA

The assessor needs to be able to identify assets and their function in the environment and then compare what they see to a certain standard. That standard is set in the security policy of the organization that owns the asset. The policy is supposed to be based on a government or industry regulation, act, or law.

Copyright © 2022 by Bruce Brown

The assessor has tools like vulnerability, compliance, and wireless scanners. However, the SCA still needs to know what they are looking at, whether it's a network, a system, or physical security, and know what assets are supposed to be protected.

Here are a few of the tasks that the CISA mentions:

- Perform security review, identify gaps in security architecture, and develop a risk management plan

- Perform risk analysis

- Plan and conduct security authorization reviews

- Verify that application software/network/system security postures are implemented as stated, document deviations, and recommend required actions to correct those deviations

- Assess the effectiveness of security controls

This book will cover the main tasks the SCA needs to do for each of the NIST 800 control families.

Copyright © 2022 by Bruce Brown

Assessment Process

All the top security frameworks have an "assess" process. ISO 27001 (international information security standard), SOX (financial security rules), PCI-DSS (credit card security rules), and many others. All of them have a robust assessment process.

You could argue that you cannot have a working security framework without an assessment process to verify security controls are in place.

International Standard for InfoSec

The international standard on which many countries base their security frameworks, ISO 27001, Information Security Management, has an assessment in the process.

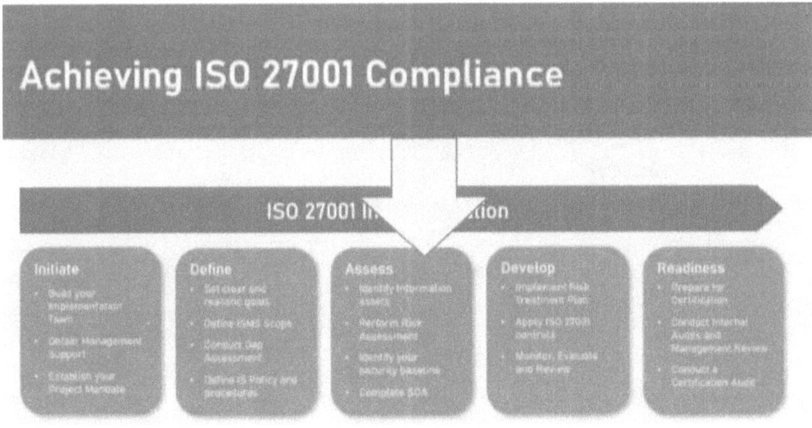

In the ISO 27001 assessment process, the organization identifies assets, performs risk assessment, identifies the baseline, and completes the statement of applicability. 27001 certification is sought after by companies worldwide, from Australia's Air Maestro to "You Verify" from Nigeria.

Copyright © 2022 by Bruce Brown

Imagine if you are a data storage company in Canada and want to ally with businesses in Norway because you know there is a huge market for what you do. Showing that you have a 27001 certification lets them know the level of rigorous security process you have gone through. They will know that your organization is assessed regularly.

Assessments and InfoSec for Money

Many frameworks help protect money transactions. The two most popular in the United States are SOX and PCI-DSS.

SOX is short for Sarbanes-Oxley. It comes from an act passed in 2002 to protect investors from fraudulent financial reporting by corporations. SOX includes information security management and risk assessments. The Sarbanes-Oxley Act of 2002 was based on several large organizations committing fraud against investors. The risk assessment for SOX assessments for the internal control framework (ICF) includes:

- Specifying appropriate objectives
- Identifying and analyzing risks
- Evaluation of fraud risks
- Identifying and analyzing changes that could affect internal controls

Copyright © 2022 by Bruce Brown

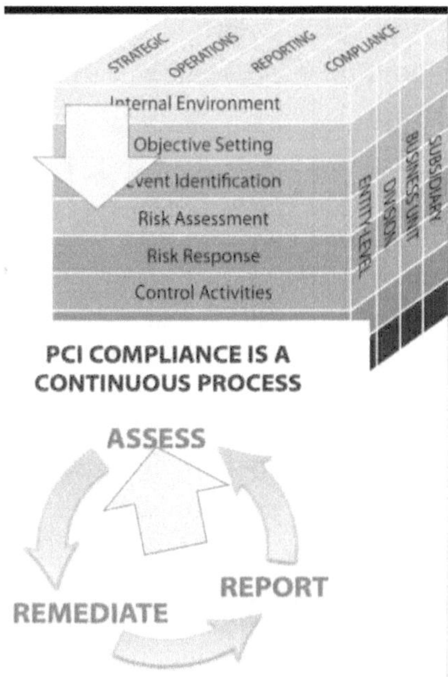

Payment Card Industry Data Security Standard (PCI DSS) is a set of security standards created by Visa, MasterCard, Discover, and other major credit card services. The set of security standards includes best security practices for any organization with a point-of-sale system that collects credit card data. PCI DSS has three steps in its assessment process:

- Identify all locations of cardholder data

- Taking an inventory of IT assets

- Analyzing vulnerabilities that could expose cardholder data

NIST 800 Assessment Overview

This book will focus on the NIST 800's implementation of security control assessments. This process is very similar to the other security frameworks. The NIST 800 security control assessment process includes the following:

Copyright © 2022 by Bruce Brown

- Preparing the assessment – Determine what type of assessment will be done, what will be needed, and who will be needed.

- Developing the assessment plan – Create a security and privacy assessment plan and share this with stakeholders.

- Conducting the assessment – Coordinate with the stakeholders on what has been agreed upon in the assessment plan and document the assessment.

- Analyzing the Assessment Report Results – Take the documented results and create a security assessment report (SAR). The security assessor will analyze the results and present them to the organization.

- Post SCA – The assessor will present the assessment results to the organization's leadership, focusing on the main issues.

Assessment Regulations

The NIST 800 security control assessment process is based on the NIST 800-37 risk management framework process and the NIST special publication 800-53A. An assessor can get the entire process from these NIST 800-53, 800-53A, 800-115, and other special publications.

All the NIST special publications are based on federal regulations OMB A-130 and FISMA 2014.

The Office of Management and Budget (OMB) Circular A-130 mandates that the security and privacy control assessments are based on controls selected by the agency. The assessment will verify whether the controls are implemented correctly, operating as intended, and effectively satisfying requirements.

According to OMB A-130, the organization must maintain a near real-time snapshot of the system's threats and prepare for the most likely security incidents. The organization determines the

Copyright © 2022 by Bruce Brown

security control assessment's type, rigor, and frequency. The level of the assessment should match the importance of the information system. In other words, a classified weapon system and a public webserver will not have the same level of security assessment scrutiny. The classified weapon system will have a significantly harder assessment where the assessor looks at more controls in a more comprehensive and detailed way.

Federal Information Security Modernization Act of 2014 (FISMA) is the United States legislation that sets up the guidelines and security standards to protect federal information systems. This law mandat3es that organizations conduct annual independent evaluations on each major system. These evaluations test the effectiveness of the information security policies, procedures, and practices. FISMA also points to the Inspector General Act of 1978, which has some agencies assigned an Inspector General. For some organizations that do not fall under this law, the head of the organization is still supposed to have an independent assessment annually for certain systems. The FISMA document refers to the security control assessor as an "auditor." Please note that some industries and organizations separate the terms auditor, assessor, and validator. FISMA also calls assessments "evaluations." For the context of FISMA, these terms are used interchangeably unless otherwise stated.

FISMA explains that National Security Systems are treated differently. National Security systems process, store, or transmit intelligence or military information used to protect the nation. With these systems, there is often more at stake than just money and branding. Sometimes human lives, a country's credibility, and much more are at stake.

According to FISMA, these systems require all organizations with an NSS to have evaluations performed only by an entity designated by the head of the agency in a way that will ensure the

Copyright © 2022 by Bruce Brown

protection of the information at a level that matches the importance of the system. This will be done at least annually but can be conducted more often by the heads of the agency.

For more on FISMA, find the document on *www.congress.gov*

RMF and Security Controls

The RMF process and associated control interpretation are covered in Books 1 & 2 of the NIST 800 Cybersecurity series. We will briefly review the process within context of the assessment.

This book addresses all the control families in NIST special publication 800-53, Security and Privacy Controls for Information Systems and Organizations.

The security control assessment methods are covered in NIST 800-53A, Assessing Security and Privacy Controls in Information Systems and Organizations.

The special publications cover all the requirements of OMB Circular 130 and FISMA.

The NIST 800 risk management process is designed so that not all 1000+ controls need to be covered during assessments. From the beginning, the system going through the RMF process only uses the controls necessary to fit the importance of the system. The NIST special publications would say, "information systems have a categorization that allows selection of security controls commensurate with their impact level." This is a fancy way of saying a federal financial and security system responsible for paying FBI agents across the country will have more security controls than an isolated Department of Agriculture workstation with mostly public data. The risk management framework ensures that each system has security controls to match the data's importance. So, classified data

Copyright © 2022 by Bruce Brown

will have more protection than a web server with publicly available data.

The first thing that must be done in the RMF process is to determine the levels of security objectives of the system. The security objectives are the following security concepts:

- Confidentiality – restricting who has access to the information.

- Integrity – ensuring the original information is not manipulated or corrupted.

- Availability – making the data accessible to those who need it.

From the perspective of a security control assessor, we are evaluating whether the system has confidentiality, integrity, and availability via fully implemented security controls.

For the organization, the security objectives determine the impact level of the system and the security categorization. A system can be Low, Moderate, or High. The NIST security controls are selected based on the impact level of the system. Here are the security control families that will be addressed:

AC - ACCESS CONTROL

AT - AWARENESS AND TRAINING

AU - AUDIT AND ACCOUNTABILITY

CA - ASSESSMENT, AUTHORIZATION, AND MONITORING

CM - CONFIGURATION MANAGEMENT

CP - CONTINGENCY PLANNING

IA - IDENTIFICATION AND AUTHENTICATION

IR - INCIDENT RESPONSE

MA - MAINTENANCE

MP - MEDIA PROTECTION

Copyright © 2022 by Bruce Brown

<u>PE - PHYSICAL AND ENVIRONMENTAL PROTECTION</u>

<u>PL - PLANNING</u>

<u>PM - PROGRAM MANAGEMENT</u>

<u>PS - PERSONNEL SECURITY</u>

<u>PT - PERSONALLY IDENTIFIABLE INFORMATION PROCESSING AND TRANSPARENCY</u>

<u>RA - RISK ASSESSMENT</u>

<u>SA - SYSTEM AND SERVICES ACQUISITION</u>

<u>SC - SYSTEM AND COMMUNICATIONS PROTECTION</u>

<u>SI - SYSTEM AND INFORMATION INTEGRITY</u>

<u>SR - SUPPLY CHAIN RISK MANAGEMENT</u>

Source: csrc.nist.gov

In this book, we suggest assessing each NIST 800 control family. This book is not a replacement for the NIST 800 publications but a guide to help navigate.

Control Assessments Overview

The CA control assessment family specifically addresses assessments in the risk management framework process. CA-1 covers the policy and procedures for control assessments being done by the organization for continuous monitoring, security certification, and authorization. CA-2 is specifically for control assessment and addresses the need for an organization to conduct regular assessments. There are two main points of the CA-2 assessment:

- Continuous monitoring is done within the organization

- Annual assessment (federally mandated)

- Track changes

- Applicable experts to do the assessment

Copyright © 2022 by Bruce Brown

For CA-2, the organization ensures that control assessors possess the required skills and technical expertise to develop effective assessment plans and to conduct assessments of system-specific, hybrid, common, and program management controls, as appropriate. The required skills include general knowledge of risk management concepts and approaches a comprehensive knowledge of and experience with the implemented hardware, software, and firmware system components.

Organizations assess controls in systems and the environments in which those systems operate as part of initial and ongoing authorizations, continuous monitoring, FISMA annual assessments, system design and development, systems security engineering, privacy engineering, and the system development life cycle. Assessments help organizations meet information security and privacy requirements, identify weaknesses and deficiencies in the system design and development process, provide essential information to make risk-based decisions as part of authorization processes, and comply with vulnerability mitigation procedures.

CA-2 has security enhancements that address the need for different types of assessments based on the security categorization of the system.

No.	Control Name	Low-Impact	Moderate-Impact	High-Impact	Privacy Control Baseline
CA-1	POLICY AND PROCEDURES	CA-1	CA-1	CA-1	CA-1
CA-2	CONTROL ASSESSMENTS	CA-2	CA-2 (1)	CA-2 (1) (2)	CA-2
CA-3	INFORMATION EXCHANGE	CA-3	CA-3	CA-3 (6)	
CA-4	SECURITY CERTIFICATION				
CA-5	PLAN OF ACTION AND MILESTONES	CA-5	CA-5	CA-5	CA-5
CA-6	AUTHORIZATION	CA-6	CA-6	CA-6	CA-6
CA-7	CONTINUOUS MONITORING	CA-7 (4)	CA-7 (1) (4)	CA-7 (1) (4)	CA-7 (4)

Copyright © 2022 by Bruce Brown

At the moderate-impact level, the system will require CA-2(1) independent assessors, which includes:

- Impartial assessments – teams or groups with no conflict of interest

- Authorizing officials to determine the level of independence

According to the NIST 800-53, an independent assessor conducts an impartial assessment of systems. "Impartial" means that the assessors are free from any conflicts of interest involving the assessed system's development, operations, sustainment, or management. Resources can do Independent assessments within or outside the organization if they are impartial to the system.

For High-Impact systems, CA-2(1) and CA-2(2) security enhancements are required. CA-2(2) is a "special assessment." A special assessment includes verification and validation, system monitoring, insider threat assessments, malicious user testing, and other forms of testing. These assessments can improve readiness by testing the operational readiness and performance of the system as well as the security and privacy.

Many weapons systems that I worked on had special assessments done. The system was so important that we would conduct assessments, validate, and verify that it worked as it was designed. So, we would have the operational users on the system processing real data as we assessed the implemented security features. We would run a network or configuration scan first to verify that the system had all applicable controls in place, then we would run the system as if it was in production. There would be quality assurance people there checking all mission requirements.

The organization can also contact third-party organizations and conduct assessments, CA-2(3), and external organizations.

Copyright © 2022 by Bruce Brown

Reasons for Assessments

There are many reasons that an organization will conduct an assessment. New threats to the organization or industry may prompt an intense round of social engineering and phishing campaigns. If they discover old vulnerabilities within the enterprise, it might prompt a risk assessment with intense network scans. Or the head of the organization may ask for an Ad Hoc assessment that has not been scheduled.

There are three main reasons that an organization will want to have assessments done:

- Continuous monitoring
- Initial implementation of a System
- Major Changes

We will touch on each one of these.

Continuous Monitoring

Continuous monitoring is a key piece of the NIST risk management framework process. This is where the organization reviews the security controls in the environment. This is done with regular network scans, security checks, and assessments.

The NIST 800-137, Information Security Continuous Monitoring (ISCM) for Federal Information Systems and Organizations, gives comprehensive guidance on monitoring. All the suggestions come from the FISMA and OMB regulations. The organization determines the frequency of monitoring. They also determine which controls are monitored and how frequent they will be.

Monitoring is a catalyst for conducting assessments, but it's also something that the SCA checks during independent third-party assessments. As an SCA, we do many of the things addressed in the NIST 800-137 addresses. NIST 800-137 guides establishing a

Copyright © 2022 by Bruce Brown

continuous monitoring strategy, implementation of monitoring, and the possible automation of the continuous monitoring process.

Initial Implementation of a System

When a system is first setup, and security controls are implemented, assessments must be done. An impact assessment is conducted on proof-of-concept systems or systems isolated from the production environment. This ensures no major vulnerabilities can be exploited when the system goes live. The assessment also checks to ensure the system is operating as planned. Putting out a system with no assessments is a huge mistake, even if it is a simple stand-one system with very low risks and exposure.

Major Changes of a System

This major change will require a fresh assessment if a system goes from Microsoft to the Red Hat Linux operating system. This might require a new assessment if the network nodes have completely new operating systems installed on the switches and routers. Other examples include a new firewall and physical location, from on-site server farms to cloud infrastructure. Anything where all the security controls will have to be re-installed or double-checked.

Some examples where there are no major changes include small application updates, operating system patches, and adding new office apps.

What Will be Assessed?

Often when people think of assessments, they think of network scans, but there is way more to assessments. There are different aspects of the organization that must be assessed. Some of the areas of the organization that can be assessed include (but are not limited to):

- Physical assessments
- Policy and Procedures

Copyright © 2022 by Bruce Brown

- ◉ Application Assessment
- ◉ PCI assessment
- ◉ HIPAA assessment
- ◉ Firewall rules assessment
- ◉ Risk Assessments
- ◉ Network Assessments

Types of Assessments

Another misconception about assessments is that they are all high-level Federal Inspector General audits from third-party badasses.

NO.

Most assessments are conducted in-house by the organization itself. As we discussed, continuous monitoring and major changes are two main reasons assessments must happen. Many of these changes are happening by the cybersecurity personnel assigned to the system. The assessment is carried out to ensure that the controls are implemented. Once they implement the controls, stand up a new system, and reconfigure an old one, an assessment is necessary because something drastic has changed. In these cases, they will conduct a "self-assessment." This is where the organization is checking itself. Assessments are the eyes and ears of the organization.

Self-Assessments are done in conjunction with many different organizational processes, such as configuration management, security and privacy impact determinations, incident response, and the system development life cycle.

During the change control and configuration management process, assessments are often conducted after the system engineering or system administrators have made major changes. The cyber security team will conduct an impact analysis which sometimes includes a self-assessment to determine the risk level of the changes implemented.

Copyright © 2022 by Bruce Brown

During incident response, after a system has been hacked, the organization contains or removes the threat; one of the things they need to do is assess the affected system and any systems connected to it to see if the threat has been contained effectively and if they vulnerability can still be exploited.

Self-Assessments are also done throughout a system engineering lifecycle. After a system is designed, it needs to be assessed, and during ongoing maintenance, it needs to be continuously assessed. Self-assessments are some of the most important activities an organization can do.

Copyright © 2022 by Bruce Brown

Assessment Preparation

During the preparation phase, the SCA focuses on the target of the assessment and requirements rather than the family of controls. The target of the assessment could include the organization's assets, processes, or documentation. The assessment targets have attached controls, points of contact, locations, missions, and business functionality. The preparation depends on the requirements of the organization.

NIST Security Control Assessor Process

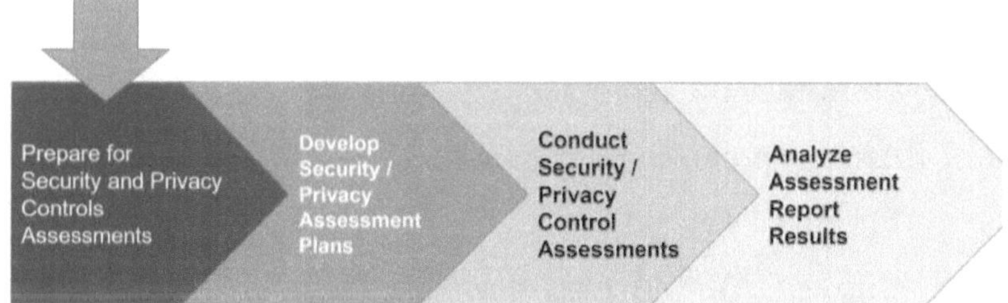

NIST Security Control Assessment Process

Here is a quick overview of the entire SCA process.

1. **Prepare the Assessment** - Determine what type of assessment will be done, what will be needed, and who will be needed.

2. **Develop the Assessment Plan** - Create a Security / Privacy Assessment Plan and share this with stakeholders.

3. **Conduct the Assessment** - Coordinate with the stakeholders what has been agreed upon in the plan and conduct and document the assessment.

Copyright © 2022 by Bruce Brown

4. **Analyze Assessment Report -** Review the results and share them with the stakeholders.

The preparation step will make or break the assessment. As with anything in life, "success favors the prepared."

Organizations Assessment Requirements

The assessment comes from the needs and requirements of the organization. The SCA cannot do anything without knowing the exact requirements.

If the organization is looking for an independent, object assessor, then the organization will need to do the following things before the assessment can happen:

- Select the assessor
- Ensure assessment fits the policy
- Determine the scope and objectives
- Arrange points of contact
- Inform all stakeholders
- Ensure SCA everything they need

For self-assessments, the organization will rely on the cybersecurity professionals who are assigned to the system to perform the required evaluation of the system. Cybersecurity professionals should take the time to understand the assessment requirement before they start. Since they are working within the organization, this won't be hard. For more on self-assessments in the preparation phase, go to "Self-Assessment Preparation."

Copyright © 2022 by Bruce Brown

Select the Assessor

The organization must select the appropriate assessor or assessor team that fits their needs.

For example, if the organization needs an evaluation of its disaster recovery and backup systems, the best person for this job is someone familiar with this. If a network scan is a part of the assessment, the most qualified person will be a subject matter expert in network assessments.

The organization must know its environment to choose the right people for the assessment. For this reason, they must include technical leads familiar with how everything works and the solutions being used. They cannot rely on upper-level management alone to determine what will be assessed and the requirements. They need to rely heavily on technical people.

Ensure the assessment fits the policy

It's up to the organization to ensure that the assessment is done within the confines of the policy that covers security and privacy controls. This includes the frequency and types of assessments that can be done and the needs of each system.

Sometimes organizations have part of the enterprise with operational systems that would be interrupted if a scan was done at certain times per day.

Policies might include rules that require certain restricted areas to have special permission to access before the assessment.

Objectives and Scope

The organization must ensure that the systems are ready and in the right step of the risk management framework before the assessment. This means the security controls' categorization, selection, and

Copyright © 2022 by Bruce Brown

implementation (by NIST 800-37) should be made before the assessment.

Knowing the system's current status, security posture, and environment will help the organization determine the objective and purpose of the assessment that needs to be done.

Is it a routine continuous monitoring assessment only requiring in-house cyber security personnel? Is the assessment isolated to just a documentation review? Is an inspector general assessment necessary for all systems in the agency.?

It will be the organization that will need to identify exactly what needs to be assessed. This includes the scope and range of the IP addresses that will be scanned, the personnel (if any that will be interviewed), and the documents within the scope to be reviewed for the system. As an SCA, we need to get this information before we can start.

For cybersecurity professionals in an ISSO role conducting a self-assessment, they should be familiar with the scope of the assessment right down to the specific controls that need to be addressed and the time frame of the assessment. If not, they should know whom to contact within the organization to get this information.

Arrange points of contact (POC)

The organization will need to arrange the points of contact for each set of assets and controls that will be covered. These points of contact will be the people doing the work daily on the assets or having access to the resources that the SCA will need to do their job. This includes inside groups like the common control providers. An example of a common control provider would be the physical security team that is outsourced to control access to the facility. If this organization is necessary for the SCA's assessment, then it needs to ensure they are included in the list of POCs.

Copyright © 2022 by Bruce Brown

Inform all stakeholders

The organization will need to contact all the stakeholders affected by the assessment. System administrators and engineers on the systems may need to be points of contact for the SCA or ISSO conducting the assessment. System operators might also need to be informed if the assessment will impact their ability to conduct daily missions and business. Management will need to be right in the middle of what is happening to help get the word out on that assessment. Informing all relevant parties will ensure no one is surprised, and relevant subject matter experts can be ready for any questions or tests the ISSO or SCA will have during the assessment.

The organization is responsible for providing everything the SCA needs to conduct the assessment. This includes policies, procedures, network diagrams, access to networks to scan, and anything else necessary.

Ensure the SCA has everything they need

The organization can minimize miscommunications by allowing direct contact with the subject matter expert managers or representatives that will be needed during the assessment. These POCs will provide the proper documentation, meet with the assessor to identify any complex issues that might arise during the assessment, and give deeper insight into the systems being assessed if necessary.

Assessor / Assessor Team Preparation

Before the assessor can begin the security assessment plan, they will need the following:

- Understand the concept of operations
- Organizational structure
- Point of contacts
- Artifacts

Copyright © 2022 by Bruce Brown

Understand the Concept of Operation for the System

The assessor better understands the system's mission, functions, and business processes. This will give context to why certain things are the way they are. The organization may need a legacy system because it supports an old mission being replaced. A certain unconventional configuration may be used because of a special business process the organization requires.

Knowing why the system exists and seeing high-level network diagrams and system security plan data will give the SCA a picture of the system's structure.

Organizational Structure

The SCA should understand the organization's entities responsible for developing and implementing the controls and supporting systems.

Points of Contact

By meeting the appropriate organizational officials and POCs, the SCA can understand what the system needs, the type of assessment, the scope, and the difficulty level.

Artifacts

The SCA will need certain artifacts before they even start. These include (but are not limited to):

- Policies
- Procedures
- System security plan
- Designs & diagrams
- previous assessment results
- security configurations of relevant systems

Copyright © 2022 by Bruce Brown

- configuration of security tools such as firewall and router settings
- After action reports
- Minutes from configuration management meetings
- Authorization packages
- Ongoing maintenance of controls

Later in the book, we will detail the recommended POCs and artifacts for each NIST 800 control family.

Self-Assessments Preparation

Most assessments done on a system will be self-assessments. Self-assessments are from the internal cybersecurity professional as an ISSO, GRC policy subject matter expert, or SCA.

To focus on the assessor role, we will refer to the cybersecurity professional conducting this task as either an SCA or an assessor.

All of the above requirements from the organization still apply. But it will be much easier for the internal ISSO and SCA to do this because they closely relate to the organization's mission and business processes.

During a self-assessment, the SCA will know where to find all of the necessary artifacts, know whom to contact for most systems, and they will know where all the skeletons are.

If you are conducting a self-assessment, you will still need approval from management within the organization, and stakeholders need to know what is happening.

Aside from the level of access during assessment preparation, self-assessments are usually more informal. Independent third-party assessments usually have specific templates that must be used, a certain number of meetings with key players that must be available,

Copyright © 2022 by Bruce Brown

and required deliverables that are expected at the end of the security control assessment. The meetings are very formal.

Conversely, a self-assessment will have meetings and deliverables only necessary to do the work. If self-assessment is required for configuration changes, the meetings might consist of just typical configuration and change controls. I have done some self-assessments that reviewed the security control statements in the system security plan (SSP). In these cases, my only coordination was one-on-one meetings with a system administrator to ensure the data provided in the SSP was still accurate.

Self-Assessment for Major Changes

Configuration management and change controls sometimes require a self-assessment to ensure security controls are still in place effectively. These will require the system admins, developers, or engineers who developed the system and made the changes. The deliverables that will be needed include the following:

- Scans before and after the changes
- Network vulnerability
- Plan of action and milestone documents (if necessary)
- Meeting minutes
- Impact analysis

Requirements will vary from organization to organization, so the assessor must do their homework.

Self-Assessment for Security Incident

Depending on the security incident, the organization may require a self-assessment. The self-assessment will determine whether the threat can still exploit the vulnerability. The incident response team will be necessary points of contact. The deliverables may include the following:

Copyright © 2022 by Bruce Brown

- Scans that allow a before and after status (if necessary)
- Incident response report
- Network vulnerability scan
- After-action report
- Forensics data of the breach (if any)
- Root cause analysis report
- Analysis of audit logs (if any)

Self-Assessment for Continuous Monitoring

One of the most informal self-assessments are done for continuous monitoring. Assessments are a regular part of continuous monitoring. Some self-assessments for continuous monitoring focus on the controls rather than the assets.

The necessary points of contact will vary for this one. Sometimes you need to coordinate with network administrators; sometimes, you need the server administrators, and sometimes it's privacy managers. It just depends on the set of controls being assessed. Sometimes, the ISSO conducting the SCA must let management know they are reviewing controls. They review implementation statements within the applicable governance, risk, and compliance database or content management systems (such as eMASS, Archer, Xacta, or others). Information system security managers or senior security personnel usually need to know what is happening. Some of the artifacts and tasks necessary include:

- System security plan updates
- Privacy impact analysis (if necessary)
- Network vulnerability scans
- Documentation review

Copyright © 2022 by Bruce Brown

There are too many artifacts and tasks to name here. And it's best to focus on the types of continuous monitoring that will dictate what artifacts are necessary.

Types of Continuous Monitoring Tasks

Many tasks and techniques can be used to continuously monitor an organization's self-assessment. Here are a few:

- social engineering
  - internal phishing campaign
  - physical security checks and challenges
- cyber threat intelligence
- penetration testing
- application security scans
  - web application assessment
  - source code assessment
- cloud assessments
- verification and validation
- policy, procedure, and process assessment

Copyright © 2022 by Bruce Brown

Security Assessment Plan

The security assessment plan is developed by assessors or someone performing SCA tasks. It is sometimes called a security and privacy assessment plan, SAP, or assessment plan.

According to the NIST computer security resource center, an assessment plan defines the objectives for the controls assessment and a detailed roadmap of how to conduct an assessment.

This plan is based on the requirements of the organization, and it is tailored specifically for their needs. The SCA can follow a basic template of what is supposed to be in an SAP, but there is no one size fits all plan I can give you. The security and privacy plan will cover the assessment's "who, what, when, where, why, and how". The SCA documents the plan and then reviews and approves it for the organization for independent third-party assessments.

Overview of a Security Assessment Plan (SAP):

The security assessment plan usually includes privacy controls. If the organization needs it, they could have a separate assessment plan that addresses privacy.

It should be noted that systems that process, store, or transmit personally identifiable information will require a separate privacy process consisting of a privacy threshold analysis (PTA) and privacy impact analysis (PIA), documented and updated frequently determined by the organization. The privacy assessment process is usually a self-assessment process completed by the organization. But the SAP does not exclude any privacy controls associated with the system having the assessment. Privacy issues will be documented in the security assessment report if they come up.

Copyright © 2022 by Bruce Brown

The SAP provides the objectives for the security and privacy control assessments and details a roadmap. The assessment plans may be developed as integrated or distinct depending on organizational needs. For example, there could be a separate assessment plan that addresses network scans and another that addresses physical security assessments, a separate one that details a policy and procedures review, and so on.

During the preparation stage, the organization and the SCA will determine what goes into the plan. The following steps are considered by the assessor and the organization when developing plans to assess the security and privacy controls:

- Determine which assets on which sites will be part of the assessment within the systems authorization boundary.

- Determine which security and privacy controls and control enhancements are to be included in assessments based on the contents of the security plan and privacy plan (or equivalent document if the controls to be assessed are non-system-based common controls) and the purpose and scope of the assessments.

- Select the appropriate assessment procedures based on security or privacy controls and control enhancements.

- Choose the selected assessment procedures (e.g., select appropriate assessment methods and objects and assign depth and coverage attribute values).

- Develop additional assessment procedures to address security requirements or controls not covered by NIST special publication 800-53.

- Optimize the assessment procedures to reduce duplication of effort and provide cost-effective assessment solutions.

- Finalize assessment plans and obtain the necessary approvals to execute the plans.

Copyright © 2022 by Bruce Brown

Security and Privacy Assessment Plan Format

Some security assessment plans start with a cover sheet. This front page can have the organization's name, the system's name, the version, and the date of the document.

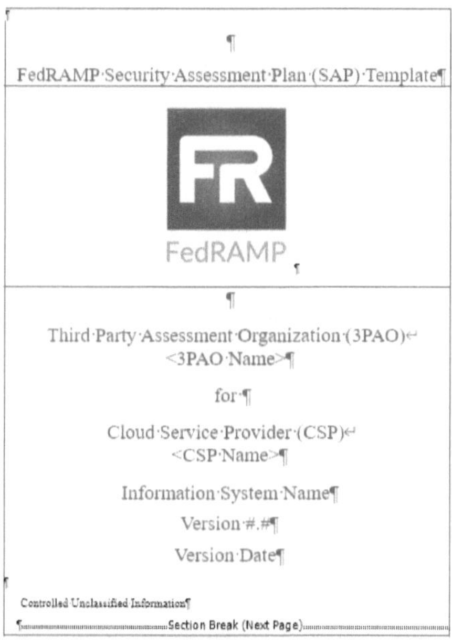

The cover of the assessment plan is optional. It depends on the form and format that the organization has. This could be the assessor's format or the organization's format.

It depends on how they do it. If the SCA comes from an upper-level agency, they will have a format they use for every lower-level organization they go to. Self-assessments don't usually waste time with a cover sheet, and the format will be as simple as possible.

Formats I have seen include a document generated by a governance, risk, and compliance database / content managers like RSA Archer or eMASS, which has the system's name, the date the assessment will be done, and the controls scheduled to be assessed. And that's it.

Copyright © 2022 by Bruce Brown

Upper-level, outside agencies performing a formal audit have a much different set of assessment documents. For example, Inspector General (IG) audits, and Department of Homeland Security (DHS) formats resemble a booklet with a coversheet and attached appendices with all the scan data.

Security and Privacy Assessment Plan Purpose

Because there are so many reasons, occasions and events that spark an assessment, it is important to provide the purpose of the assessment inside of the SAP.

This could be part of the scheduled internal continuous monitoring, an annual IG audit, or a step in the change control process. Whatever it is, it should be mentioned in the notes of the SAP so that others working on the document can follow up, and upper-level management will be able to differentiate this assessment from all the others. Remember, organizations are doing several types of assessments and scores of business and mission systems in the organization, so the more explanation you have, the better.

The purpose also helps create a context for the assessment itself.

Sample Purpose Statement (Self-Assessment)

The purpose of this security control assessment is annual continuous monitoring established by [OrganizationA] for [SystemA]. This follow-up assessment addresses the remaining NIST 800-53 security controls and reviews all associated risk response documentation, such as risk acceptance, plan of action, and milestone documents.

Sample Purpose Statement (Third-Party Assessment)

The Department of Homeland Security (DHS) will independently audit [OrganizationA] business and mission systems' external network connections. The security assessment plan appendix A will detail IP addresses and hostnames.

Copyright © 2022 by Bruce Brown

Security and Privacy Assessment Regulations & Background

This part of the SAP will briefly summarize the main federal, state, or industry regulations that give authority and guidance to the assessment process. Federal security assessment plans might mention FISMA and OMB. Any relevant country, county, or state information system regulations would be cited alongside any necessary industry regulations. Industry regulations might include HIPAA for healthcare, PCI DSS for organizations using credit cards, and ISO 27001 for international systems.

Sample Security and Privacy Assessment Regulations

The [OrganizationA] security control assessment is being done by the Federal Information Security Modernization Act of 2014 (FISMA) and the Office of Management and Budget (OMB) Circular A-130 laws. This legislation was put forth to ensure the protection of federal information systems.

Security and Privacy Assessment Process and Methodology

This section outlines the assessment methodology to verify and validate that the management, operational, and technical controls are appropriately implemented. The assessor might summarize what network scanning tools (if any will be used) or explain that penetration testing will be used.

To evaluate management and operational controls, the assessor must explain that interviews and document evaluations will be part of the assessment.

Security and Privacy Assessment Scope

The scope of the SAP is important. The name and description can be put here, but more importantly, this section defines the limits of the assessment. It defines what is scanned and where if there are multiple physical locations.

Copyright © 2022 by Bruce Brown

This section might list all the information systems or the range of devices assessed. The scope can have a separate appendix that lists all the systems to be assessed, references the range of IP addresses, or just refer to the systems if all of the individual systems on the system are clearly defined and identified by the organization.

The organization needs to agree on the scope before the assessor proceeds.

During self-assessments, the cybersecurity professional conducting the assessment will typically name a specific number of systems, IP addresses, or a group of controls being checked.

Assessment Assumptions and Limitations

Assumptions refer to beliefs or expectations taken for granted during the security assessment process. These may include assumptions about the assessment's scope, the assessment team's knowledge and skills, the availability of resources, and the accuracy and completeness of any documentation or information provided. It is important to clearly define these assumptions in the plan so that stakeholders understand the basis for the assessment and can evaluate the validity of the results.

Limitations, on the other hand, refer to any factors that may affect the accuracy or completeness of the assessment. These may include technical limitations, such as the inability to access certain systems or data, or organizational limitations, such as restrictions on using certain assessment tools or techniques. It is important to identify these limitations in the plan so that stakeholders are aware of any constraints that may affect the assessment results and can take them into account when interpreting the findings.

It is important to note that the assumptions and limitations section is not intended to justify any shortcomings in the assessment process. Rather, it is a means of providing transparency and context

Copyright © 2022 by Bruce Brown

for the assessment so that stakeholders understand the scope and boundaries of the analysis.

In summary, the assumptions and limitations section of a security assessment plan is a critical part of the document that provides transparency about the process and identifies any constraints or boundaries that may affect the accuracy or completeness of the assessment. It is important to clearly define assumptions and limitations in the plan so that stakeholders can evaluate the validity of the results.

For templates of the Security Control Assessment process, go to: www.convocourses.com/assessortemplates

Copyright © 2022 by Bruce Brown

Conduct the Assessment

It's time to get to work after an agreed-upon security assessment plan establishes the assessments who, what, when, where, and how.

This can be done on-site, remotely, or some combination of the two. For example, the network scanning portion and documentation review of the assessment (if applicable) can be done remotely. The physical security check and wireless assessment will be conducted on-site. It just depends on how they have planned this out during the creation of the security assessment plan. It's often more cost-effective to conduct as much of the assessment remotely as possible. Onsite assessments require more time, money, and resources for the organization.

What Professional Assessors Do

Managing expectations and staying within the assessment's scope sets professional-level assessors from amateurs. Give yourself more time than you need to complete the assessment. If you think it will take two days on-site, ask for three or more days, and try to do as much work as possible before you get there.

Do not go over the days you need. If you ask for two days and then need three and a half, you can expect the client to say something about this. Every minute that they escort you is money for them. It's better to ask for more time than you need and do it in less time.

Stay within the scope of the assessment. One of the worst things you can do is assess systems, not on the security assessment plan. God forbid you find some critical vulnerabilities on systems you were not even supposed to scan and count it against them! The client will go ape.

Copyright © 2022 by Bruce Brown

Conducting self-assessments

Self-assessments conducted by in-house cybersecurity professionals are much more informal. The assessor will have an easier time creating an assessment schedule that is in line with stakeholders because it's much easier to communicate with them and there is less pressure.

Since self-assessments are usually triggered by mundane internal activities such as routine continuous monitoring, or major system changes, its more relaxed. There is also less scrutiny as the results will likely only be viewed internally. This is very different than independent third-party assessments pushed from higher level organization. However, the same methods and process can be used in both self-assessment and third-party assessments.

Assessment Methods

The NIST 800-115, Technical Guide to Information Security Testing and Assessment, is a good resource for the SCA.

According to 800-115:

An information security assessment determines how effectively an entity being assessed (e.g., host, system, network, procedure, person—known as the assessment object) meets specific security objectives.

In other words, a security control assessment determines how well the security features of a system or organization are done. The assessor looks at the objects in the organization and system to do this.

The NIST 800-53A describes the things you will examine as "objects." Security policies, procedures, host system configurations, and people you interview are all "objects."

Copyright © 2022 by Bruce Brown

There are three main methods used to assess whether security controls have been implemented:

* Examine

* Testing

* Interviews

The SCA examines, tests, and interviews objects (documents, systems, and organization resources and assets) to determine if security controls have been implemented well.

The SCA looks at what the organization has in place and compares it to assessment objectives. Assessment objectives are what the assessor should see for compliance or the expected results. The assessor can find expected results in the NIST 800-53A, the organization's requirements, best security practices, or some combination.

Assessment Method: Examine

The "examine" assessment method is observing, checking, reviewing, inspecting, studying, or evaluating the objects. In the case of examining, some examples of "objects" are documentation, host system configurations, information system, procedures, people, networks, and any other resources that enable security control.

The examination method is part of almost every security control assessment, whether looking at policies or evaluating a test's results to determine the controls' effectiveness.

The NIST 800-53A has a list of objects to select from for each security control.

AC-04(01)-Examine	[SELECT FROM: Access control policy; information flow control policies; procedures addressing information flow enforcement; system design documentation; system configuration settings and associated documentation; list of security and privacy attributes and associated source and destination objects; system audit records; system security plan; privacy plan; other relevant documents or records].

Copyright © 2022 by Bruce Brown

Assessment Method: Interviews

Interviews are discussions with the personnel who know about or work with the system or security control in some way. An interview can assess certain operational security controls more effectively than a test or examination. For example, gauging how well the subject matter experts know their processes would be best evaluated in an interview.

Some questions can give a deeper insight into how the organization and its system are being protected.

When users, subject matter experts, and managers of the system go on record with certain statements, it can cover a lot of ground for the assessment quickly. Their statements are called "attestations" and can be used to pass or fail a security controls implementation.

Assessment Method: Testing

Testing is best for technical system controls. This is where the assessor interacts with the information system to see the behavior. Normally, the SCA will have the subject matter expert (system administrator, firewall administrator, network engineer, etc.) get on the system and type requested commands. This is the best-case scenario since the subject matter expert knows their systems better than anyone, and they should have the level of access necessary to conduct the hands-on test.

Testing is logging in, performing system restores, and system backups, using different kinds of accounts to access configurations, opening the event logs, displaying firewall rules, demonstrating system capabilities, and much more. It's any direct interaction with the system to see the outcome.

Copyright © 2022 by Bruce Brown

Expected Results

Regardless of the method used to evaluate the effectiveness of the control, the assessor is comparing the outcome of the examination, testing, or interview with what the organization is supposed to be doing.

What they are supposed to be doing is documented in the organization's policy. If they don't have a policy, plan, or document that details the restrictions and rules, then it is documented in the federal, industry, state, or local regulations, directives, or laws.

We will go into greater detail about conducting assessments for each control family.

Copyright © 2022 by Bruce Brown

Security Assessment Report (SAR)

The security assessment report documents all your findings from the security control assessment. The SAR gives an executive summary of what was done, an overview of the total risk level, identifies each vulnerability found, and suggests how to remediate each finding.

The SAR can be a spreadsheet, a pdf, a secure web page, or some combination of media. I have seen it even include a PowerPoint presentation. The format of the SAR depends on the organization.

A more comprehensive assessment will produce an entire package that may include dozens of pages and the results of network scans. No matter how long the document is, it needs a summary for upper-level management, an overall risk level, and a breakdown of each vulnerability, also known as a "finding".

Importance of the SAR

I was late delivering an assessment report to one of two of my clients. Client A was not in a rush to get the assessment because they didn't need it yet. They needed more time to figure out what to do with some of the vulnerabilities they knew they had. But Client B lost their mind. They needed the security assessment report for some internal quarterly reports tied to corporate bonuses. Client B contacted their CEO and my manager.

The moral of this story is to never be late with your reports. Give yourself ample time to conduct the assessment and assemble the report.

Copyright © 2022 by Bruce Brown

Assessments are important to the organization. It's the eyes and ears of the organization. Without it, they are groping around in the darkness. In the case of Client B, they were relying on the assessments I created to figure out how much funding to give to manage risk.

The layout of a typical SAR

I. Executive Summary

- A brief overview of the risk assessment process
- Key findings and recommendations for risk mitigation
- Conclusion and next steps

II. Introduction

- Purpose and scope of the risk assessment
- Methodology and approach used
- Assumptions and limitations

III. Risk Assessment Process

- Preparation for the assessment
  - Define scope and objectives
  - Identify assets and stakeholders
  - Establish risk tolerance criteria
- Conducting the assessment
  - Identify and assess threats and vulnerabilities
  - Analyze potential impacts and the likelihood of occurrence
  - Determine the level of risk and prioritize actions
- Maintaining the assessment
  - Monitor and update risk assessment regularly
  - Incorporate feedback and lessons learned

Copyright © 2022 by Bruce Brown

- Communicate risks to stakeholders

IV. Results and Findings

- Summary of identified risks and vulnerabilities

- Analysis of potential impact and likelihood

- Prioritized list of risk mitigation recommendations

- Assessment of residual risk after mitigation

V. Conclusion and Recommendations

- Overall assessment of risk level

- Summary of key findings and recommendations

- Next steps for risk management and mitigation

VI. Appendices

- A detailed description of the methodology and analysis

- Supporting documentation, such as risk matrices and threat models

- Glossary of key terms and acronyms

For NIST 800 assessor templates, go to:
convocourses.com/assessortemplates

Copyright © 2022 by Bruce Brown

Post-Assessment

Post-assessments are not documented in the NIST 800 series; however, in my experience, this is done at almost every organization. After the assessment is conducted and a security assessment report is generated, there is a process of review, SAR modifications, and delivery that is supposed to happen.

For self-assessments that are done as a part of continuous monitoring, the post-assessment might be as simple as reviewing the results, getting a peer review, and submitting them to the relevant manager for further review. This depends on the level of self-assessment and the internal processes. But conducting assessments for third-party organizations is different.

For third-party assessments, where you are an independent assessor for an organization, the post-assessment is a bit more involved.

- Review the assessment report
  - Always allow someone else on the team to review it. This is called a peer review, and it is super important
- Deliver the report to the team to allow them to respond to the results
  - Give them a few days to look at the results and explain or point out inaccuracies
- Take a look at the organization's response and feedback
- Present the findings to the stakeholders

The assessment report is delivered to the organization, and the organization that manages and owns the system being assessed gets a chance to respond. The ability to respond needs to be in the report

Copyright © 2022 by Bruce Brown

itself. Everyone needs to know that the report is not final until the client's security team has had the chance to respond.

They need a chance to respond because some findings may be false positives or already known and documented.

Responding to False Positives

A false positive is where a scanner detects a flaw where there is none. The vulnerability scans detect weaknesses based on a set algorithm that will extract data in the system files or compare the version of an application it finds on the system with the most current secure version that should be on the system (for example).

Examples of vulnerability scanner false positives may include vulnerabilities identified that are not exploitable, misidentified software or operating systems, or system configurations that the scanner misinterprets as security risks.

As an assessor, you may not notice all the false positives. Your focus is to detect weaknesses across multiple systems; there is limited time to do this.

As an assessor, your interpretation of the findings focuses on whether the scan ran correctly on the right systems. You may not have time to dive deep into each finding. The assessor needs to give the cybersecurity team and system owners time to review the results and explain (if necessary). The cybersecurity team and system owners know their system better than anyone, so they will know that they updated a certain patch and added that to the assessor's report.

Known Documented Issues

If the organization has been doing its self-assessments as a part of its continuous monitoring, it will develop a risk response for things it could not fix within its prescribed vulnerability remediation time. A risk response is acknowledging the risk and explaining how the

Copyright © 2022 by Bruce Brown

organization will handle that risk. There are several kinds of risk responses:

- Plan of Action and Milestone (POAM) – A POAM is a document that deferrers the fixed actions of weakness by making a plan that is tracked over time
- Risk Acknowledge – Also known as "risk acceptance," are documents where the organization states that they know about the risk, but they have a justification of why it's there. They have minimized the risk by protecting the system in other ways.

Other documents will share risk with other organizations, exceptions, risk transfers, etc. The point is that the organization can respond to the assessment findings with documents that justify how the risk is managed in another way besides remediation.

Post-Assessment Meeting

Meetings are not always necessary. Internal self-assessments don't usually have a meeting. If there is a meeting, the assessor should summarize the main point of the findings and include any of the organization's responses (if any).

After everything is complete and the organization has responded, the SCA can meet with all the relevant stakeholders. The relevant stakeholders will be the primary points of contact (usually the cybersecurity team), IT management if they are available, and a C-Level executive (or representative). The C-Level executive should be the Chief Information Officer, Chief Information Security Officer, authorizing officer, or anyone who signs the authorization package. Because this is whom the report will go to.

Copyright © 2022 by Bruce Brown

AC - Access Control Family Assessment

When we look at the AC, Access Control, family from a security control assessors' perspective, we need to see if the organization controls the logical access to its assets. Our first step is to identify what assets have the business essential function. Then we want to see if they are protecting network access, wireless access, remote access, and mobile phone access to those essential functions.

This control family will take longer than average because several controls rely on account management. For example, if badging is connected to an account, physical and personnel security (PE and PS controls) will depend on account management. Audit logs (AU controls) require that certain events identify the account. Other controls that rely on account management include identification, authentication, and privacy controls, just to name a few.

As Assessors, we want to look at the following controls in the AC family:

- AC-1, Policy & Procedures
- AC-2, Account Management
- AC-17, Remote Access (if applicable)
- AC-18, Wireless Access (if applicable)

I am not telling you to exclude all the other controls in the AC family. I am just saying that as a minimum, we want to assess these four keystone controls that give insight into the organization's overall access control practices.

Copyright © 2022 by Bruce Brown

Identify the Essential Functions for Access Control

The focus is on the access control process. The focus is not on a golden server in a restricted area with sensitive information that holds all the essential functions. Focusing on the access management process will identify issues on all the systems with essential functions. It's still helpful to know where the most important mission essential functions are because that will allow the assessor to evaluate the level of risk to the organization.

As an SCA we are not fixated on *just* one server or even a group of systems; we are looking for the organization's process for access controls. We might use a sampling of systems across the enterprise. We only do this to observe the behavior that the organization has configured on the systems and the process that they have put in place to protect access.

We assess a set of important DNS servers or a critical database. Realistically, if the organization does not have access controls, an attacker could potentially access those mission-essential functions from an end user's system via wireless, remote access, or other methods.

Examination of Account Management Controls

The account management process must be documented and clearly defined in a policy and explained in a procedure. The policy should be current and signed by upper management. Just make sure the policy is not expired. If it is three years old or signed by leadership that is no longer around, point this out in the risk assessment report. The procedures should explain how access management is currently being done. Procedures will sometimes reference old tools and techniques that are no longer used.

Copyright © 2022 by Bruce Brown

As a bare minimum, the policy should address the following:

- Account roles & Role-based Access (AC-3)
- Account creation and termination (AC-2)
- Account monitoring
- Unsuccessful logon attempts
- System Use Notifications

Sometimes these account management policies & procedures are addressed in multiple documents. The types of documents may include:

- Overall security policy
- Access control policy
- Personnel Termination or Transfer policy (human resources)

Other Evidence of Account Management

The SCA can also observe a list of active system accounts, lists of disabled system accounts, and lists of groups and members of those groups. Active Directory and other account management tools allow the system administrators to export accounts.

Copyright © 2022 by Bruce Brown

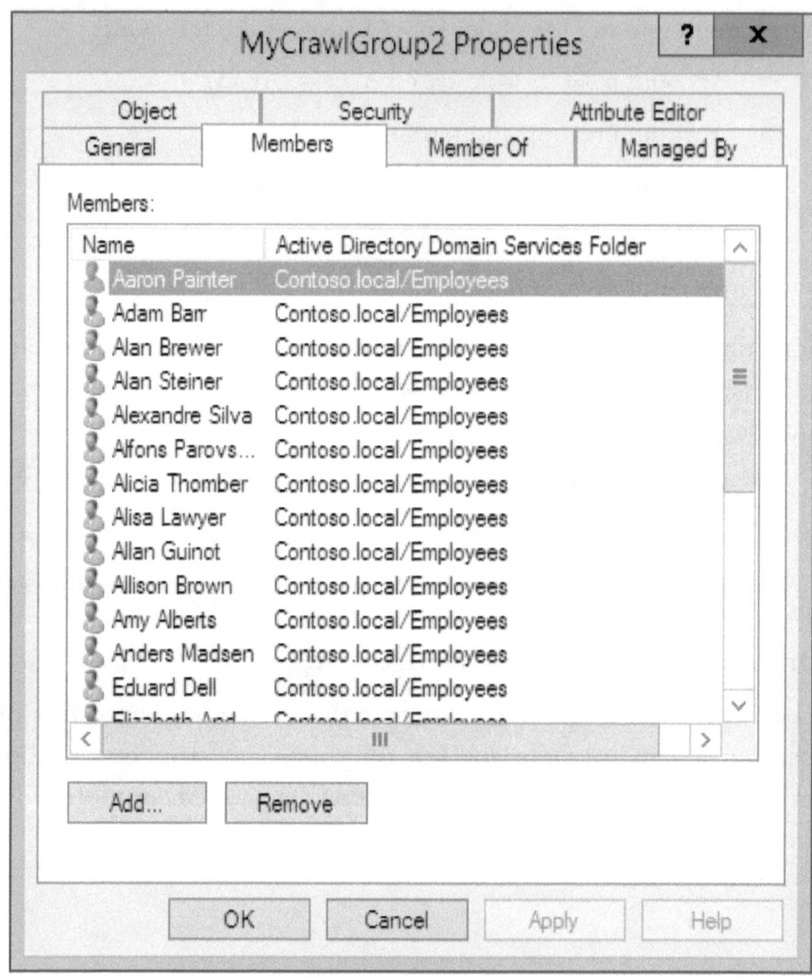

Members of a group

Copyright © 2022 by Bruce Brown

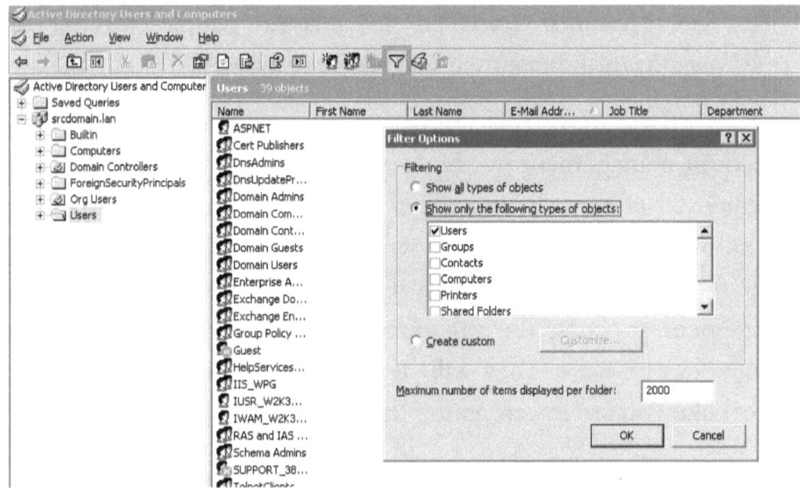

Export Users or Groups from Active Directory

Interview for Account Management Controls

You will want to talk to the point of contact with some idea of the account management process. This could be a cybersecurity professional, a system administrator, or whoever is well-versed in the organization's account management. In my experience, the best people to talk to are the professionals creating, maintaining, and deleting accounts. Their knowledge is so deep that after only a few questions, I don't have anything else to ask. Here are some questions that can be asked about access management:

- What applications do you use for account management (Active Directory, LDAP)?

- What types of accounts do you have (administrator, guest)?

- How and when are accounts removed?

- What is the process for a new person to get an account?

- Does the security team have different account permissions than the system administrator team, or are they the same team?

Copyright © 2022 by Bruce Brown

- Are accounts reviewed to ensure people leaving the organization have their accounts removed?

These are all questions that imply that the organization not only has an account management but has a process that is followed. If this is implemented effectively and the SCA talks to the point of contact who knows how it works, these will be easy "softball" questions. If the SCA is talking to someone who does not know the account management process, the organization does not have an account management process. They will start sweating and stuttering, and it will feel like you are interrogating them.

Testing of Account Management Controls

The SCA can test whether the organization uses access management. One of the ways this can be done is by logging in to a system that can demonstrate the use of an account.

There are a few methods that can be used:

- Log on to the system as a guest
- Attempt to access administrative tools as a guest
- Have the point of contact logon as a standard user
- Have the point of contact login as a privileged user
- Attempt to log in with no credentials
- Attempt to log on with random credentials

The expected results of the test depend on what the organization says they are doing in its security policy.

These are only some methods that can be used to test account management in an organization.

Red Flags of Access Management

If you see a bunch of accounts from people who have left the organization, this is a big problem. It means the organization might

Copyright © 2022 by Bruce Brown

not have the removal of accounts in their process. These accounts become forgotten and can be exploited by attackers if not removed.

Green Flags of Access Management

When an organization has a regular review process of accounts, this is very good. Every account adheres to a strict lifecycle, and any loose ends are captured during the periodic review.

Examination of Wireless Controls

This only applies if the system that is being assessed is accessible from wireless networks or has Wi-Fi or Bluetooth enabled. It will need to have restrictions on the wireless.

Restrictions for wireless will be documented in a policy and procedure. Wireless documentation should establish the configuration and connection requirements. An example would be a policy that mentions the mandatory use of WPA-Enterprise and restrictions on guest accounts, and the use of Bluetooth. Other documents should guide implementation.

Bluetooth is often forgotten and overlooked. There should be restrictions in writing because the users will think nothing of bringing in their own Bluetooth devices and connecting them to the organization's systems.

Often the organization and users are unaware of common Bluetooth hacks and vulnerabilities, which include:

- Bluejacking – broadcasting a message to all Bluetooth-enabled systems.
- Bluebugging – establish a backdoor on a phone or laptop via Bluetooth.
- BlueBorne – attack device (Armis) exploits the system through Bluetooth
- BlueSnarf – pairs with a system to steal data

Copyright © 2022 by Bruce Brown

The organization should have a policy that limits what can be connected to its infrastructure.

An organization that is fully aware of Bluetooth hacks will have some of these restrictions documented:

- Turn off Bluetooth when not in use
- Do not pair with untrusted devices
- Do not keep sensitive information on a Bluetooth device
- Use a strong password/PIN
- Update to the latest Bluetooth versions
- Enable Bluetooth security features

The Wi-Fi policy should address some of the most common vulnerabilities, such as:

- Default Wi-Fi router configurations
- Rogue access points
- SSIDs protection
- Use of WEP

Testing of Wireless Controls

Many assessments have components that can be conducted at one site or even remotely to determine much of what is happening at the other sites. For example, network scans and document reviews can be done remotely. But wireless testing must be done on each site, like physical assessments. The range of the wireless and its overlap with other wireless being broadcast are all part of the assessment.

There are three parts to the wireless assessment:

Step 1: Talk to the wireless owners

Step 2: Conduct the wireless Internally & Externally

Step 3: Gather the data

Copyright © 2022 by Bruce Brown

Step 1: Talk to the Wireless owners

Before you walk around the organization's site with wireless scanning equipment, you will need approval from upper management and the site you are going to. The SCA and the target organization need to agree on the scope and requirements of the assessment at the specific site. An SCA should never conduct a wireless assessment without written consent from management and the specific site's acknowledgment. There may be special configurations that you need to know about. For example, at one site I visited, the organization had a partner organization with wireless and Bluetooth enabled systems on the facility's north side. I needed to exclude data from the other wireless network. These were details that the site manager told me and had not been included in the overall security assessment plan.

Step 2: Conduct the wireless Internally and Externally

You can use a few devices and apps to conduct the scan. These include the following and will change over time:

- Stormpad – CEH raspberry pi device that scans all Wi-Fi and Bluetooth devices on the network
- Pwn Pad – wireless and Bluetooth scanning device
- Blue Hydra – Bluetooth scanning application
- Wi-hawk – tool for auditing IP addresses on wireless routers
- Bitdefender Home Scanner – scans Wi-Fi networks
- Fing App – scan network from a mobile app

There is a variety of wireless scanning devices and apps can be used on the organization's sites. Let the client know what tools will be used.

Whatever scanning solution you get, ensure it can gather data on all SSIDs, access points on Wi-Fi, and potential Bluetooth vulnerabilities in different areas of the site.

Copyright © 2022 by Bruce Brown

You will need to walk around the inside of the facility, protected areas, and the outer perimeter. You will require a point of contact to escort you to restricted areas. Do not conduct Bluetooth scans outside. Bluetooth has a range of 10 meters, so if you conduct a Bluetooth scan outside the facility, you will pick up things like people's personal phones, watches, and wireless headphones.

Step 3: Gather the Data

The scanner will pull in data from the wireless enterprise. It will be gibberish to most people if it is not put in a clear, understandable, and organized format highlighting the overall risks to the organization.

The document should clearly show what the risk is and where it is. I should list the SSIDs, and Bluetooth detected (if that is part of the scan).

Some tests might include:

Have the point of contact sign in to the wireless while conducting the scan:

- Access the guest account while conducting a scan
- Attempt to connect to the wireless with no credentials
- Attempt to pair with Bluetooth devices
- Setup a rogue access point to see if it is detected (needs approval from the organization)
- Attempt to connect to the secure wireless from outside the network.

Interview of Wireless Controls

The SCA will talk to the IT professionals responsible for maintaining the wireless or anyone at the organization who knows how it is set up. This may include cybersecurity professionals in an ISSO role, network administrators, network engineers, or site facility managers.

Copyright © 2022 by Bruce Brown

The types of questions might include the following:

- How do enterprise users access the WIFI?
- How do guests access the WIFI?
- Is the guest network separate from the employee wireless?
- Does the organization have rogue access detection?
- What type of encryption is used?
- Does the organization have restrictions on the use of Bluetooth?

Red Flags of Wireless

A completely open wireless network would be an instant red flag for the wireless and the entire network. If you find one, you have to wonder if the organization is allowing direct access from that open network to internally protected assets. An open wireless network will have no access control at all.

Using obsolete and compromised encryption, such as WEP, is also a red flag. WEP is Wired Equivalency Privacy. WEP can be cracked easily, allowing attackers to see all data on the network.

An organization with absolutely no control over Bluetooth has no idea of the risks of the technology. They don't have any policies or procedures; they don't pay attention to legacy Bluetooth in their environment. This is not good.

Green Flags of Wireless

If the organization has a wireless network with the highest level of encryption and authentication, it means that someone there knows about threats to the wireless.

Copyright © 2022 by Bruce Brown

Examination of Remote Access Controls

If remote access is allowed, the organization should explain that they allow remote access to the system being assessed. The policy documentation is usually high-level, leaving more technical details to engineering and procedural documents. Look for configuration and connection requirements and implementation guides for each kind of remote access (if they have multiple). You are looking for encryption via virtual private networks (VPN).

The SCA will ensure the remote access documentation reflects the organization's current work. This can be in the overarching security policy or a separate remote management document approved by upper management.

Interview for Remote Access Controls

In my experience, remote access assessments are usually done with interviews, observing scanned data, and documentation. The SCA should talk to someone who knows and uses the remote access systems that are in place. Preferrable a technical person or group who will know things like the encryption and vendor and not just the process. Here are some suggested interview questions:

- Does this system allow remote access?

- What is the product used for remote access? (This question is to determine if a remote access solution is still supported)

- What is the encryption used for remote access? Does it use a VPN?

- Who is allowed to have remote access? All users?

- Are regular users and privileged users allowed to have remote access?

In the questioning, we are trying to see if they have a process that limits remote access and if they are implementing the limitations that they have documented.

Copyright © 2022 by Bruce Brown

Testing of Remote Access Controls

For testing, the SCA will determine if the organizational users access the system remotely as described by the security policy. At this point in the process, the focus is on the mechanism that allows remote access. Here are some options for testing:

- Have the point of contact remotely access the organizational system being tested.

- Have the point of contact remotely connect the system with a privileged account (if possible).

- After logging in remotely, have the point of contact remain logged in to see if the connection will automatically disconnect after a certain period detailed in the documentation.

- Have the point of contact connect remotely using different types of remote access methods (if the organization has more than one method of connecting).

- Have the system administrator login into the backend of the remote management system and show how it is configured.

- Attempt to log in remotely with a guest account.

One of the issues of testing a remote connection is that sometimes the system is configured so that you cannot test this while on-site. You would have to test it from outside of the enterprise, and the assessment is usually done on-site, so observation and interview are used instead of testing.

Red Flags of Remote Access

This is not good if the organization uses end-of-life software for remote access. There are too many known exploits for remote access that target EOL software. If the organization uses weak encryption or (worse) no encryption, it might already have been hacked. The document the severity of this huge mistake.

Copyright © 2022 by Bruce Brown

Green Flags of Remote Access

An organization implementing remote access properly will not only have vendor-supported remote access solutions, but they will also use military-grade encryption like AES and end-to-end VPNs. The organization will have strict limitations on remote access, such as timeouts for inactive sessions or limitations on what systems allow remote access. Some organizations even restrict which systems are remotely accessed by whom and only at certain times of the day or night.

Examination of Access to Mobile Devices

AC controls include controlling access from a mobile device. The SCA is looking for connection requirements and connection and implementation guidance documents for mobile device system access.

A Mobile Device Management (MDM) policy can include the following:

- Laptop and notebook computers
- All smartphones (iPhones and Androids)
- Tablets
- All portable media devices

Please note that sometimes laptops and notebooks are used as components of stationary workstations and are not used as functional mobile devices. As such, notepads and laptops are part of the MDM on a case-by-case basis.

The MDM policy will apply to employees, guests, and contractors using mobile devices to access the affected system.

This only applies to systems that allow access from mobile devices to the system being assessed. For example, let's say the organization allows the regular use of mobile devices throughout the facility, but if none of these mobile devices are allowed to access

Copyright © 2022 by Bruce Brown

SystemX, the system being assessed, then access for the mobile device does not apply to the system.

There are three categories of mobile devices usage:

- Bring your device (BYOD) – allowing users to bring and use their mobile devices at the organization.

- Company-owned / business only (COBO) – the company owns the device, and it is only used for business.

- Company-owned / personally enabled (COPE) – the company owns the device, but it can be used for personal use.

Whichever categories are used should be documented, and all the restrictions noted. Some restrictions might include things like:

- Encryption for data at rest on mobile devices

- Encryption for data in transit

- Lockdown of application configurations

- Restrictions on applications

- System profile settings

- Cloud store restrictions

- Device function lockdowns

- Device supervision

- Device location tracking

Interview of Access for Mobile Devices

The SCA's questions will be centered on the organization's MDM policies and procedures.

- What department controls the mobile device restrictions?

- Who is allowed to access the system via mobile devices?

- What systems can be accessed from mobile devices?

- What are mobile devices used to access the system?

Copyright © 2022 by Bruce Brown

- What can be done on the system from the mobile device?

- Is the data on the mobile device encrypted?

Testing of Access for Mobile Devices

When the SCA is looking into using mobile devices to access the assessed system, they will compare the access to what is in the security policy. There are a few tests that can be done to determine if the organization has restrictions:

- Have a user access the system via BYOD phone (check for restrictions mentioned in the policy)

- Attempt to access the system via a mobile device not approved by the organization

- Check the system for encryption of data at rest setting or data in transit

- Attempt to download random games on the mobile device

- Check the mobile device management settings of the mobile device

Essentially, the SCA can go down the list of restrictions and requirements detailed in the documentation and test the mobile device to determine if those features are enabled.

Red Flags of Mobile Devices

I have been at an organization that uses mobile devices on their network, but they had little or no control over the devices of the VIPs (upper-level management). Worse, they didn't know what was on those phones or what authorized users were doing with them.

Copyright © 2022 by Bruce Brown

Green Flags of Mobile Devices

A great MDM program will have full remote control and monitoring of all devices (without exceptions). They will educate all authorized users on what they can and cannot do on the organization's mobile devices.

Mormon Hacker: Church of Latter-Day Hacks

"So, what I do is I set up a free wireless access point. I put it outside in public places." My hacker friend's face lit up with glee. "You'd be surprised how many people sign up for it. And this device can capture all information on all Wi-Fi in the area."

"Why do you do it?" I asked him. We were both members of the local Information System Security Association. He looked like a Mormon. He wore slacks and a button-up long-sleeve shirt. He had the face of a young politician the majority would vote for without knowing his stance. But he had the morals of the hacker group Anonymous.

He was so anti-establishment that I was sure he had a safe house in the middle of the Rocky Mountains and maybe some laptops rigged to explode if he had to destroy evidence of unauthorized access to multiple governments.

I did not want to know, but I asked, "Do you hack their accounts?"

"No," he said. "I just do it for fun."

I have no way of knowing if what he was saying was true.

This guy is on LinkedIn. For my safety, I will not be revealing his identity.

But you have probably seen him pop up if you have ever searched for pen testing or hacking. All he does is hack stuff. He is one of three terrifyingly smart cybersecurity people I know personally

Copyright © 2022 by Bruce Brown

who could be supervillains if they wanted to. By the grace of a higher power, they have not turned to evil.

This hacker dude was doing something in 2007, now known as a "Wi-Fi pineapple."

It is a way to automate gaining access and gathering data on people's accounts. This method of going access is now common knowledge. Anyone can buy a kit off the internet and set one up at a bank, on a base, in a store, or wherever.

This is only one of the reasons why access controls and user education are so important. SCAs must test to ensure the organization has access control processes in place for wireless and account management, remote access, and mobile devices.

Copyright © 2022 by Bruce Brown

AT – Awareness and Training Control Assessment

Awareness Training or AT controls cover security and awareness training for all business or mission systems users.

For security control assessments, we need to find evidence that the organization has a training program that is robust enough to fit the size and complexity of the network or system we are assessing.

Our evidence includes emails showing recent training activity, screenshots of computer-based testing, and a spreadsheet with a breakdown of the training schedules.

We want to make sure the training fits the environment.

For example, it would be reasonable for a five-computer local area network with only three active users to have all training conducted, tracked, and recorded via email yearly. But manually tracking and recording annual security awareness training via email for an enterprise of 400 mixed-mode systems (Linux and Microsoft servers) and 1500 users would not make sense. There is no way they could effectively track all the training by email alone.

The AT family of controls can cover a lot of ground:

- Privacy
- Insider threats
- Cybersecurity
- Phishing

As assessors, we are looking for their process covered in their documentation, whether the training matches the environment, whether there is any specialized training they are supposed to have,

Copyright © 2022 by Bruce Brown

and whether they have role-based training. The following controls are important:

- AT-1, Policy & Procedures
- AT-2, Literacy & Awareness Training
- AT-3, Role-Based Training

Other AT controls will apply to organizations, but these three assessors focus on the training process.

Required Training Assessment

Some industries require specialized training. For example, systems in the healthcare industry might have required HIPAA training. Military and intelligence-based organizations might have training for handling classified information. Retail and customer service could have required training for protecting customer privacy data or PCI / DSS credit card data.

Other specialized training might include:

- Records Management training (law enforcement)
- Financial data protection (financial sector)
- Government Compliance training (government)
- Phishing Campaigns
- Privacy
- Insider threat

If there is specialized training, the SCA must pay attention to these in the policy. Once it is observed in the policy, determine if this training is being done.

Copyright © 2022 by Bruce Brown

No.	Control Name	Low-Impact	Moderate-Impact	High-Impact	Privacy Control Baseline
AT-1	POLICY AND PROCEDURES	AT-1	AT-1	AT-1	AT-1
AT-2	LITERACY TRAINING AND AWARENESS	AT-2 (2)	AT-2 (2) (3)	AT-2 (2) (3)	AT-2
AT-3	ROLE-BASED TRAINING	AT-3	AT-3	AT-3	AT-3 (5)
AT-4	TRAINING RECORDS	AT-4	AT-4	AT-4	AT-4
AT-5	CONTACTS WITH SECURITY GROUPS AND ASSOCIATIONS				
AT-6	TRAINING FEEDBACK				

AT Control Family

Examination of Security Awareness Training

The organization should have some sort of document that explains the security awareness training program, the frequency of the training, and how the training is conducted. This might be a policy, a training plan, a procedure, or perhaps all these things with a set of training manuals.

The assessor is making sure that there is an overarching document that points out the security awareness training. They will look at this policy or plan and see if the organization has reviewed it in the last year. They will also need to check out any recent training records showing that training is being done annually. Training should teach the user to conduct basic security practices at a bare minimum.

For large, high-impact systems that require a lot of system administrators, the assessor will look at the training records for specific roles.

A list of acceptable artifacts includes:

- Screenshot of completed training
- Spreadsheet of users' training schedule
- Emails of training completion

Copyright © 2022 by Bruce Brown

- Training certificates

The assessor just needs to see if the organization is doing training each year for basic security awareness. There should also be training in place for specific roles. For example, cybersecurity professionals will need training that fits their role if they are on staff. Role-based training is required in addition to security awareness training.

Interview for Awareness and Training

In addition to observing training records and policies, the SCA may interview system users to determine if the organization has an active training program.

They can interview a standard user to ask the following:

- What type of training do you receive?
- Is there security awareness training in the organization?
- When was the last time you did cybersecurity training?
- Can I see evidence of your training?

For privileged users or special access users, the SCA might ask the following to determine role-based training compliance:

- What is your role in the system? (System administrator?)
- Do you have training for your role?
- When was the last time you had training on those administrator tasks?

Red Flags of AT Controls

The assessor can see a lack of training during interviews. If the subject matter expert on the system does not have basic knowledge of the system that they are assigned to, the assessor needs to ask for training records. There is a possibility that the assessor is just talking to the wrong person (which happens all the time). But if they have talked to several people in the organization and quite a few are ignorant of the

Copyright © 2022 by Bruce Brown

processes and system they support, then there is a good chance the training is inadequate. Other red flags:

- No training records at all
- No indication of a training site or training material

Green Flags of AT Controls

Highly knowledgeable subject matter experts who have done several assessments will be confident. It will be like they rehearsed. They will not only know the system they are assigned to but be familiar with the current processes and why they do them. Good organizational training is homegrown and not just generic, so it teaches the local process to protect the system. They will have basic security awareness training and role-based training.

I Blame the Army

"Airman Smith, when does the assessment start?" I didn't take my eyes off the screen. I was almost done with my troop's evaluation. I was supposed to finish it by the close of business that day. Meanwhile, I was waiting for the assessment team to arrive so I could escort them on-site.

"Are they here yet? Do we need to pick them up at the gate?"

"The assessment already started, sir," Smith shook his head. "Yeah, did you get this email? Looks like they are already in the network. We have a breach."

I didn't even save my work. I jumped out of my chair and over to his desk to look at his computer. A notification was sent out by the security operation center informing all information technology operators of a breach and the start of the Red Team exercise.

The assessment team was testing our network by hacking it. They'd gained approval to conduct the penetration test.

Copyright © 2022 by Bruce Brown

They were penetrating us hard and deep and fast… There is literally no other way I can word it. We were screwed. Now I needed to know how screwed we were. I would need to let Master Seargent Tenison know about this, so I needed more details.

I called my contact at the security operations center.

A gruff low voice answered the phone, "Staff Sergent Mattheson, Incident Handling Security Ops, may I help you sir or ma'am."

"Sergeant Mattheson, this is Sergeant Brown at the Information Management Office," I took a deep breath and continued. "I see the SOC just sent out a breach for the assessment team. Can you give me a little more info? How did they get in?"

Sergeant Mattheson laughed, "Phishing attack."

"A phishing attack?!" I cursed. "Who clicked the damn link!? Everybody has been informed and trained. We send out tests and training every other month. What unit?"

"Everybody has been trained," Matheson agreed. "Everybody except the Army. Some Army helicopter unit out of Bragg. I guess they don't have to do our training."

"The Army." I sighed. "Say no more."

Copyright © 2022 by Bruce Brown

AU – Audit and Accountability Control Assessment

Audit logs are critical to the organization's cybersecurity, ongoing maintenance, and troubleshooting. The audit logs are the text files from the servers, routers, laptops, desktops, software, and all systems. The text gives a summary of what is going on with the system. If a server reboots, logs are created, so the system administrators know when and why the system restarted. If the collaborative software suite crashes, the help desk technician collects and reviews error logs to determine why the software is not working. When the routers and the web server are running slow, the network engineers and cybersecurity analysts can use the audit logs to determine if there is a denial-of-service attack.

AU, audit, and accountability controls ensure that the event logs are turned in, tracking the right things, and being reviewed occasionally.

As an assessor, we are focused on some of these AU controls:

- AU-1, Policy & Procedures
- AU-2, Event Logging
- AU-3, Content of Audit Records
- AU-6, Audit Record Review, Analysis, and Reporting
- AU-9, Protection of Audit Logs
- AU-11, Record Retention

Copyright © 2022 by Bruce Brown

Examination of Audit and Accountability

The organization should have a documented process for system logging. The policy and procedures will detail what is being logged. It would be useless to log everything because it would be too difficult to manage and monitor all the logs from all the systems.

Instead, look at the documents that point out the types of logs collected and on what systems.

As an SCA, it is not our place to tell them what they should log. Our job is to ensure they have documented the need for logging and identified their requirements. This covers AU-1, audit, and accountability policy.

Once we see their requirements, we must ensure they collect what they say they are logging. We need to check out their logs. If their policy states, "Organization XYZ ensures all failed login attempts are logged," then we need to see that in the event logs of their system.

Example of audit logs:

Keywords	Date and Time	Source	Event ID	Task Category
Audit Failure	4/22/2020 2:32:31 AM	Microsoft Windows secur...	4625	Logon
Audit Failure	4/22/2020 2:32:31 AM	Microsoft Windows secur...	4625	Logon
Audit Failure	4/22/2020 2:32:31 AM	Microsoft Windows secur...	4625	Logon
Audit Failure	4/22/2020 2:32:31 AM	Microsoft Windows secur...	4625	Logon
Audit Failure	4/22/2020 2:32:31 AM	Microsoft Windows secur...	4625	Logon
Audit Failure	4/22/2020 2:32:31 AM	Microsoft Windows secur...	4625	Logon
Audit Failure	4/22/2020 2:32:31 AM	Microsoft Windows secur...	4625	Logon
Audit Failure	4/22/2020 2:32:31 AM	Microsoft Windows secur...	4625	Logon
Audit Failure	4/22/2020 2:32:31 AM	Microsoft Windows secur...	4625	Logon
Audit Failure	4/22/2020 2:32:31 AM	Microsoft Windows secur...	4625	Logon

Copyright © 2022 by Bruce Brown

Audit Logs – Logon Failure

Recent audit logs will tell the SCA that the organization has audit logs that match its event log requirement. This is covered in AU-2 event logs.

Depending on how deep the assessment needs to go, the SCA might look at logs from each type of system in the assessed environment. In my experience, both performing assessments and being assessed, the SCA looks at the logs of the primary mission and business systems. They are not looking at the MS Office, printers, or other peripheral logs, just supporting the main mission. However, the logs from endpoint devices of users can be very useful in tracking down cyber attacks and troubleshooting.

Record retention can be assessed by looking at where logs are collected. Logs are stored on the local hard drive of systems by default. This applies to all computer systems, including internetwork devices (switches, firewalls, routers), mobile devices, servers, and desktops. Organizations that collect a lot of logs usually send all logs

Copyright © 2022 by Bruce Brown

to a centrally managed location. The SCA should examine these logs, looking for current timestamps.

Interview for Audit and Accountability

In addition to observations, the SCA can interview the security operations center to determine if the audit logs are being reviewed. The assessor will need to speak to the appropriate people. In this case, it would be the information system security officer, cybersecurity analyst, or security operation center analyst. Questions would consist of the following:

- Does the organization collect audit logs?
- Where are audit logs analyzed?
- Where are audit logs stored?
- How often are audit logs examined?
- What types of events are logged?
- What systems are collecting events?
- How long are logs kept?

This is an opportunity for the SCA to ask about the incident response (IR controls). They can ask:

- What does the organization do if there is a security incident?
- What types of security incidents have been detected?
- What does the organization do if there is an attack or malware detected?

Copyright © 2022 by Bruce Brown

No.	Control Name	Low-Impact	Moderate-Impact	High-Impact	Privacy Control Baseline
AU-1	POLICY AND PROCEDURES	AU-1	AU-1	AU-1	AU-1
AU-2	EVENT LOGGING	AU-2	AU-2	AU-2	AU-2
AU-3	CONTENT OF AUDIT RECORDS	AU-3	AU-3 (1)	AU-3 (1)	AU-3 (3)
AU-4	AUDIT LOG STORAGE CAPACITY	AU-4	AU-4	AU-4	
AU-5	RESPONSE TO AUDIT LOGGING PROCESS FAILURES	AU-5	AU-5	AU-5 (1) (2)	
AU-6	AUDIT RECORD REVIEW, ANALYSIS, AND REPORTING	AU-6	AU-6 (1) (3)	AU-6 (1) (3) (5) (6)	
AU-7	AUDIT RECORD REDUCTION AND REPORT GENERATION		AU-7 (1)	AU-7 (1)	
AU-8	TIME STAMPS	AU-8	AU-8	AU-8	
AU-9	PROTECTION OF AUDIT INFORMATION	AU-9	AU-9 (4)	AU-9 (2) (3) (4)	
AU-10	NON-REPUDIATION			AU-10	
AU-11	AUDIT RECORD RETENTION	AU-11	AU-11	AU-11	AU-11
AU-12	AUDIT RECORD GENERATION	AU-12	AU-12	AU-12 (1) (3)	

More AU controls for Moderate and High

Testing of Audit and Accountability

Having logs enabled and collected is only half of what needs to happen with audit and accountability. The organization should regularly review the logs.

SCAs will sit with administrators to determine whether logs are reviewed, protected, and enabled. A standard user might have read-only privileges to the audit logs but should not be able to change the configuration of the event logs.

If a standard user can stop the event logs, an internal attacker could corrupt or alter the system and erase evidence of their malicious activity using regular privileges.

Copyright © 2022 by Bruce Brown

To test the audit logs, the SCA should have a privileged user open up the settings of the logs to ensure that the organization's requirements enable them.

The assessor can also have a standard user attempt to open and manipulate the log settings. This will validate that the logs are protected to comply with AU-9 protection of audit logs.

Event logs sometimes include first names, last names, phone numbers, addresses, and other personally identifiable information (PII). If PII is being collected, the assessor should observe or test the data's protection. Only authorized individuals should be able to access or modify protected logs.

Red Flags of AC Controls

Sometimes the organization will have documentation about audit logs, but the logs are disabled. This is a red flag because they know what they are supposed to do and what the assessor wants to see but have not implemented the audit log features.

Another issue I've seen is then the organization has a mixed-mode environment with two different operating systems. Sometimes they will collect logs for one effectively but not for the other. Or they will have logs only for servers and no logs for anything else, and they may have a reason for this. As assessors, we must document what we see.

Green Flags of AC Controls

A centralized security information and event management system that collects all applicable logs on the system is a good sign. It usually means they have carefully selected the logs, they are parsing them, and have a role dedicated to monitoring, analyzing, and responding. A centralized security event manager with small organizations or isolated systems might not exist. It will be enough to have a

Copyright © 2022 by Bruce Brown

documented process where they take the time to monitor the logs at a frequency determined by the organization.

AU - Audit and Accountability Resources

- NISTIR 8062, An Introduction to Privacy Engineering and Risk Management in Federal Systems
- NIST SP 800-92, Guide to Computer Security Log Management

Copyright © 2022 by Bruce Brown

CA – Control Assessment

The act of assessing the system helps validate the CA controls. CA controls cover the organization's assessments, authorization, and monitoring practices. What is left to assess is the authorization and monitoring process.

By focusing on the following controls, the assessor can get a good idea of the organization's overall compliance with CA controls:

- CA-1, Policy, and Procedures
- CA-2, Control Assessments
- CA-5, Plan of Action and Milestones
- CA-7, Continuous Monitoring

Examination of CA – Assessment, Authorization, and Monitoring controls

The SCA must observe that the policy aligns with the security framework used. Federal systems use NIST 800, but some systems might also include: CIS, ISO 27001, PCI / DSS, or other cybersecurity frameworks. Compliance with a security framework sets up the need for assessments, authorization, and continuous monitoring.

The SCA can observe the following documents to assess overall CA control compliance:

- Last security assessment report
- Last authorization package
- Continuous monitoring of policy process/procedure
- Current Plan of Action and Milestone

Copyright © 2022 by Bruce Brown

Are Security Assessments Being Done?

The assessor is observing when the last security assessment was done. If the organization has a requirement to conduct security assessments quarterly or annually, then the SCA should see that it has been done in the required timeframe. The act of conducting an assessment is evidence that the organization has a process for CA-2 – Control Assessments.

Is there an Authorization Process?

The most recent authorization package will show that the organization has an authorization process. Some organizations don't even know what that is. As the SCA, you want this process to be in an overarching plan or policy document. It is also important that the authorization package is vetted and approved by upper-level management. Usually, this is the equivalent of a CIO or CISO; within the NIST risk management framework process, this is called an authorization official (AO).

Ways to Observe Continuous Monitoring

Continuous monitoring is done in many ways on all system security aspects. Documentation, network status, physical security, personnel security, and all controls must be continuously monitored. The SCA can observe the following to determine continuous monitoring:

- View logs of recent physical security checks
- Observe the security operations center (if applicable)
- Review vulnerability management activities
- Check the dates of recent document reviews
- Determine when the last system security plan was complete

Copyright © 2022 by Bruce Brown

The SCA needs to observe if the organization checks security controls regularly.

The organization should have a plan of action and milestone (POA&M) process that tracks any vulnerabilities that cannot be fixed within the time constraints acceptable to the organization.

They may not call it a "POA&M" process, but as the assessor, you are looking for any process where vulnerabilities that take longer to fix are tracked and dealt with over time. The worst thing an organization can do is lose track of vulnerabilities and have no plan to fix them. The only thing worse is them trying to lie about it.

Sometimes, organizations do not say anything about serious risks and vulnerabilities, hoping the assessor does not find them.

This could indicate that something worse has been swept under the rug. That thing is the integrity of the network, and they are patching serious risks with HOPE. As in, they hope they don't get hacked.

If you find this as an assessor, don't get upset that the organization is hiding stuff. Focus on presenting the data effectively. Let the data speak for itself by explaining how it can be hacked.

CA – Assessment, Authorization, and Monitoring Interview

While the SCA sits with the experts responsible for assessment and monitoring, they can conduct the interview. These questions will focus on the overall process of continuous monitoring, authorization, and internal assessments. This interview must be with a subject matter expert, information system security officer, compliance officer, or equivalent because most organizational roles will not know much about how this process should work.

Copyright © 2022 by Bruce Brown

Interview questions for the assessment process (CA-2):

- How often are assessments done on the system?
- How do you determine the scope of the assessment?
- What types of assessments are done on the system?
- Who conducts the assessments?
- How often are independent assessments conducted? (CA-2(1)

Interview questions for the authorization and POA&M (CA-5, CA-6):

- When is the last time the system has approved by the authorizing official (or CIO)?
- What is the authorization process for this system?
- Who gives authorization for this system?
- Are there any open plan of action and milestones for the system?
- What is the POA&M process?

The SCA compares what the organization is doing with what they have stated in the security policy addressing continuous monitoring, assessments, and authorization. They are also evaluating if the organization has a process at all. And if they do have these processes in place, how robust is it? In some cases, the organization has an assessment process, a method of continuous monitoring and authorization, but they lack some of these tasks for the system currently being assessed.

Testing of CA – Assessment, Authorization, and Monitoring

SCAs can test the behavior of the organization's assessment and monitoring. Assessors could have the operators or system administrators demonstrate how monitoring is done.

Copyright © 2022 by Bruce Brown

If the organization has an automated monitoring tool, assessors can have them show how endpoint devices are discovered. The SCA is looking for any of the following:

- How often is this done

- If the person in the role knows how to do it

- How thorough is the monitoring process?

Testing the internal assessment process would be done the same way. The assessor will sit down with the subject matter expert who conducts regular scanning and have them run the internal scanning tool.

Red Flags of CA controls

On systems without regular assessments, you will see strange things affecting mission and essential business functions. Here are some of the things I have seen:

- Lots of end-of-life systems are exposed to the Internet

- Systems with software that have not been patched in years

- Servers that no one can identify

- Systems that should have been decommissioned months ago

- Unsupported or unauthorized software

Green Flags of CA Controls

When organizations have conducted regular risk assessments and had managers authorize what is found, the overall risk tends to be lower than average. These organizations will usually have lots of recent assessments.

CA – Assessment, Authorization, Resources

- NIST SP 800-137, Information Security Continuous Monitoring (ISCM) for Federal Information Systems and Organizations

Copyright © 2022 by Bruce Brown

- NISTIR 8011, Automation Support for Security Control Assessments

- NIST SP 800-37, Risk Management Framework for Information Systems and Organizations

- NIST SP 800-53A, Assessing Security and Privacy Controls in Federal Information Systems

- NIST SP 800-115, Technical Guide to Information Security Testing and Assessment

Copyright © 2022 by Bruce Brown

CM – Configuration Management Control Assessment

To assess the organization's configuration management, the SCA is looking for whether the organization has a program that controls the settings and system changes. The assessor needs to see if the organization has impact analysis methods and whether they employ the principle of least functionality. Does the organization have tight control over what the systems look like and how they are set up?

If they have documented network wide configuration management issues, then they are making an effort to manage the risks. If they have no answer for these issues, this is a huge red flag to assessors because a lack of configuration management shows major systemic failure that affects other aspects of the organization's security posture. The assessor should dig deeper if there is a lack of configuration management.

Some areas to focus on as the assessor include:

- CM-1, Policy and Procedures
- CM-2, Baseline Configuration
- CM-3, Change Control
- CM-4, Impact Analysis
- CM-7, Least Functionality

If the organization does these things effectively, everything else in configuration management will fall into place.

Copyright © 2022 by Bruce Brown

Examination of the Configuration Management controls

Most configuration management controls will need to be observed rather than tested. There are a few documents that the assessor should take a look at to determine if there is robust configuration management:

- Baseline documents
- Configuration management policy
- Configuration management meeting minutes
- Configuration management database
- Change control tickets
- Configuration control board document
- Security Impact Analysis
- Privacy Impact Assessment

What can be used to validate the existence and use of a configuration management process is not limited to this list. The assessor seeks evidence of the organization having meetings to modify, add, update, or remove systems. The evidence should show the regular use of a change control or configuration management process.

Observing the Baseline Configuration documents

The assessor may look at printouts of the group policy and itemized lists of all the configurations on servers, laptops, and mobile devices. Network diagrams can also be a part of established baseline documents.

As the assessor, look at the dates of the document's creation and last review. If the document has not been reviewed in over two years, that is a problem.

Copyright © 2022 by Bruce Brown

Interview for the Configuration Management controls

The people you want to talk to are those familiar with governance, risk, and compliance that can answer configuration and control management questions. The roles you want to talk to for the interview are information system security officers, compliance officers, and equivalent. Project and operational managers will also be familiar with the process because they must appear in configuration management meetings. System administrators and other technical positions will be able to answer baseline questions.

Configuration and control management questions:

- How often do you have configuration management meetings?
- When was the last time you had a configuration management meeting?
- Do you have change control meetings?
- When was the last change control meeting?
- Are the change control meetings documented?
- Are the configuration management meetings documented?
- Can I see the meeting minutes from the last change control or configuration meeting you had for this system?
- Does the organization conduct impact assessments?
- Does this system have a privacy impact assessment?

Configuration Baseline questions:

- Do you have a documented baseline for this system?
- Can I see the baseline documents for this system?
- Who maintains the systems baseline and the documentation?
- What is the process if there is a change to the baseline?

Copyright © 2022 by Bruce Brown

The assessor should take a look at the following artifacts to determine if there is robust configuration management:

- Baseline documents
- Configuration management policy
- Configuration management meeting minutes
- Configuration management database
- Change control tickets
- Configuration control board document

Test for Baseline Configuration

There are tools that allow an assessor to look at the baseline configuration of the systems. In fact, most of the top vulnerability scanners can dive deep into the configuration settings of systems. They must use credentialed scans with elevated privileges. These scans take time and resources. These assessments take extra coordination because the assessor must work with the system administrator to set up the appropriate credentials on the systems. The scan needs to be scheduled to not interfere with essential business functions.

For medium or large networks, the assessor doesn't look at every single system to determine if there are inconsistencies in the overall baseline. They look at a sample size. The sample is a percentage determined by the scope of the assessment that represents the network. If there are 1000 Microsoft desktops, 50 Red Hat Servers, and 20 MacOS systems, the assessor might scan a sample of size of 5% of each: 50 desktops, 5 Red Hat Servers, and 2 MacOS systems. There is no rule against scanning every single system in a large environment, but the time and resources will become an issue if the SCA team takes weeks to review all the data.

Copyright © 2022 by Bruce Brown

Red Flags of CM Controls

Most organizations have some sort of configuration or change management meetings because it is so hard to get anything done as a team without these meetings. However, sometimes they don't have a cybersecurity representative in the meetings. In these cases, the security person does not know what is going on. A lack of security impact analysis is another issue I have seen. When there is a major change, it should go through cybersecurity for possible scanning and analysis.

Without configuration management in place, you will see chaos. Two laptops with the same make and model will have completely different settings for users with the same role. Some of the telling signs that the organizations systems have little or no configuration management:

- The organization doesn't know what systems are on their network
- They have systems with no subject matter expert
- Lots of mission-critical servers with legacy systems
- Lots of systems with no vendor support
- Out-of-control vulnerabilities with no plan to fix them
- Standard users with administrator rights

Green Flags of CM Controls

The configuration and control management process is well documented and accessible to all stakeholders. If the assessor asks the cybersecurity representative or subject matter expert about configuration and change control meetings, they should be able to pull them up quickly.

Copyright © 2022 by Bruce Brown

CM – Configuration Management Resources

- NIST SP 800-128, Guide for Security-Focused Configuration Management of Information Systems

- NIST SP 800-124, Guideline for Managing the Security of Mobile Devices in the Enterprise

- NISTIR 8062, An Intro to Privacy Engineering and Risk Management in Federal Systems

Copyright © 2022 by Bruce Brown

CP – Contingency Plan Control Assessment

The contingency plan (CP) controls determine whether the organization can survive disasters or mishaps. This includes human errors, natural disasters, or any other threat that is likely to happen.

As an assessor, you're looking for evidence that the organization can continue to operate the essential functions when the system goes down or that they at least have a plan in place when things go wrong.

The main controls to assess for CP controls are the following:

- CP-1, Policy, and Procedures
- CP-2, Contingency Plan
- CP-3, Contingency Training
- CP-9, System Backup

Examination of the Contingency Plan Controls

The organization should have a few documents if they have an established contingency plan. They should have an overarching contingency plan document. This document covers the entire department or unit and all the systems they control. It needs to be authorized and signed by upper-level management. This establishes that they are serious enough about CP controls to have thought about it. Backups are another part of CP controls. A policy should mandate the use of a backup process on critical systems.

Copyright © 2022 by Bruce Brown

Beneath this high-level CP policy, individual procedures or guides should explain what to do if certain disasters happen. For example, there might be a procedure on what to do during a natural disaster or a system outage.

The assessor should observe the date that the document was revised. But more important than when it was reviewed is when it was used. A common bad practice is for an organization to create a contingency plan policy that they will never use.

The organization is supposed to train and practice the contingency plans and then record the session. They will perform a mock disaster or "tabletop" exercise, where they review what they do during a disaster. This exercise is recorded in a session called an after-action report.

Here are a few CP artifacts the assessor can use to validate whether the organization has a contingency plan that they are using:

- Continuity Plans/Disaster Recovery/Business Continuity Plans for the system

- Evidence of Continuity Plan/Disaster Recovery training
  - After action reports
  - Notes for the tabletop exercise

- Evidence of backup plans (screenshots, backup policy/procedures)

- Other plans to consider include (but are not limited to):
  - Continuity of Operations plans
  - Breach response plans
  - Critical Infrastructure
  - Insider threat plans

Copyright © 2022 by Bruce Brown

Interview for CP – Contingency Plan Controls

When conducting the interview, focus on whether they have used the contingency plan. Look for whether they have updated documents for CP controls (backups and disaster recovery) and the performance of the action to restore backup and recovery systems after a disaster. This could be a real-world situation where they had to use their plans or regular exercises. Here are some CP questions the assessor could ask:

- Do you have a backup process?
- What systems are backed up?
- Can I see your system backup settings?
- Have you tested your backup recovery process?
- Do you have a contingency plan or disaster recovery in place?
- When was the last time you had to use the disaster recovery process?
- Have you used contingency or disaster recovery plans during exercises?
- Can I see your notes or after-action reports from the latest contingency plan exercise?

Red Flags of CP Controls

Most organizations will have the good sense to know that contingency planning is a thing. They will have some sort of disaster recovery or business continuity that mentions it. But it's a whole other thing to do it or practice it regularly. If there is no evidence that the CP controls are practiced, tested, or conducted in some way, this is a bad sign, and the assessor should ask more questions and document the findings.

Copyright © 2022 by Bruce Brown

Green Flags of CP Controls

When the organization has recently (within the last year) tested its disaster recovery, business continuity, or continuity of operations and has documented the results, this is a good sign.

CP - Contingency Plan Resources

- NIST 800-53

- NIST 800-34, Contingency Planning Guide for Federal Information Systems - https://www.ready.gov/

Copyright © 2022 by Bruce Brown

IA – Identification and Authentication Control Assessment

For IA (identification and authentication), assessors look at the usernames, passwords, and multifactor authentication (MFA) processes and procedures. They want to know whether the organization has policies and procedures for usernames, passwords, or MFA and whether they are doing what they have documented.

A combination of testing and observation is the best way to assess the system's use of identification and authentication controls. Observation of what the security policy and procedures say about IA controls compared to what has been implemented in the baseline configuration of the system will tell the SCA most of what they need to know.

The IA family has lots of controls:

Copyright © 2022 by Bruce Brown

No.	Control Name	Low-Impact	Moderate-Impact	High-Impact	Privacy Control Baseline
IA-1	POLICY AND PROCEDURES	IA-1	IA-1	IA-1	
IA-2	IDENTIFICATION AND AUTHENTICATION (ORGANIZATIONAL USERS)	IA-2 (1) (2) (8) (12)	IA-2 (1) (2) (8) (12)	IA-2 (1) (2) (5) (8) (12)	
IA-3	DEVICE IDENTIFICATION AND AUTHENTICATION		IA-3	IA-3	
IA-4	IDENTIFIER MANAGEMENT	IA-4	IA-4 (4)	IA-4 (4)	
IA-5	AUTHENTICATOR MANAGEMENT	IA-5 (1)	IA-5 (1) (2) (6)	IA-5 (1) (2) (6)	
IA-6	AUTHENTICATION FEEDBACK	IA-6	IA-6	IA-6	
IA-7	CRYPTOGRAPHIC MODULE AUTHENTICATION	IA-7	IA-7	IA-7	
IA-8	IDENTIFICATION AND AUTHENTICATION (NON-ORGANIZATIONAL USERS)	IA-8 (1) (2) (4)	IA-8 (1) (2) (4)	IA-8 (1) (2) (4)	
IA-9	SERVICE IDENTIFICATION AND AUTHENTICATION				
IA-10	ADAPTIVE AUTHENTICATION				
IA-11	RE-AUTHENTICATION	IA-11	IA-11	IA-11	
IA-12	IDENTITY PROOFING		IA-12 (2) (3) (5)	IA-12 (2) (3) (4) (5)	

Any number of them might come up during an assessment, but the main controls to validate in the IA family are:

- IA-1, Policy and Procedures

- IA-2, Identification, and Authentication (organizational users)

- IA-4, Identification Management

- IA-5, Authentication Management

To assess these controls, the SCA can use multiple methods to validate the implementation of the controls. They can observe the IA

Copyright © 2022 by Bruce Brown

controls, test the login process, and interview the stakeholders that manage the IA process.

Examination of IA – Identification and Authentication Controls

The organization should have a policy that addresses an identification and authentication process. This can address username and password restrictions, multifactor authentication (MFA), or two-factor authentication (2FA) requirements. The documented security controls should match the minimum restrictions set by the industry.

For example, if the organization is under the federal government and they require a 20-character password, but the organization only has 16, this should be noted in the security assessment report.

Also, if the organization states in the IA policy that they only use MFA, but you observe a system with a username and password, you need to put this in the security assessment report.

The SCA can observe the following to perform the assessment:

- Documented baseline showing the username and password settings
- Username and password settings on the system
- Multifactor settings on the system
- Identification and authentication policy
- Identification and authentication procedures

Interview of IA – Identification and Authentication

During this test, the SCA checks to see if the system's behavior matches what was approved in the policy. They can also look at user rights, require banners, audit logs settings for failed login attempts, user session restrictions, and other security controls required during the login process.

Copyright © 2022 by Bruce Brown

- Do the systems use username/password or multifactor authentication?
  - This IA question to the right subject matter experts will show if multiple login methods are used on different systems. This may have already been figured out during the observation and testing methods.
- What is the password complexity?
  - The SCA is looking for the length of the password, upper- and lower-case letters, numbers, and special characters. This should match what the organization has in its policy. Any specialized system with exceptions should be documented and approved by the organization.
- Describe the MFA process.
  - Multifactor authentication comes in multiple forms: Something you have (smart card, RSA fob), something you are (retina, face, fingerprints), and something you know (PIN code, password).
- How do you log in to mobile devices? (If applicable)
  - The authentication method might differ if the system being assessed has a mobile device.
- Is the username/password or MFA process different when logging in remotely? (If applicable)
  - The remote IA controls may differ from the local login process if remote login is possible.
- Is the login process different on different operating systems? (If applicable)
  - In an environment with more than one operating system type (i.e., Windows and Red Hat), one group of systems might have different login methods with different IA controls applied.

Copyright © 2022 by Bruce Brown

Testing the IA – Identification and Authentication

The SCA can test identification and authentication with the organization's subject matter experts. This might be the system administrators or the cybersecurity specialists who know what is going on with the login process and have access to show the system's behavior.

To test IA, the SCA can perform the following or have the subject matter expert do the following:

- Attempt to log in with no credentials or false credentials

  - This is to observe if the organization has established identification and authentication on the system and what the system does when there is a failed login attempt (IA-2 and IA-3).

- Log in as a standard user and attempt to access administrative tools

  - This tests access controls (AC). Once identification and authentication are established, each user should have restrictions on what is accessed based on their roles. Regular users should not have the same access as a privileged user (AC-3)

- Login with multifactor authentication credentials (if applicable)

  - The SCA observes the MFA behavior to determine if it matches the policy (IA-2).

- Have the system administrator login to the identification and authentication manager

  - If the organization has a centralized method of managing the identification and authentication process, the settings can be validated there (IA-2, IA-3, IA-4, IA-5).

During this test, the SCA checks to see if the system's behavior matches what was approved in the policy. They can also look at user rights, require banners, audit logs settings for failed login attempts,

Copyright © 2022 by Bruce Brown

user session restrictions, and other security controls required during the login process.

Red Flags of Identification and Authentication

A lack of multifactor authentication is a bad sign unless the system cannot do MFA for some reason. A few others are:

- Shared usernames and passwords (privileged accounts)
- A system with no username and password is necessary
- Allowing weak passwords
- No naming convention on usernames

Green Flags of Identification and Authentication

An organization that uses username and password sparingly on the assessed system is great. They are making an effort to move to integrate MFA everywhere.

Copyright © 2022 by Bruce Brown

IR – Incident Response

For Incident Response (IR) controls, the SCA will need to review whether the organization has a process that covers the system they are assessing.

Organizations usually have a security policy covering incident response, which is good. But the assessor is focused on the target system they are assessing. Does the existing incident control documentation cover the system within the scope?

The assessor needs to verify that if the target system has an incident, there is a plan and process in place for it. In most cases, the organization's overall incident response plan will cover the assessed systems.

The incident response process should cover the system being assessed:

- Prepare – organization identifies the most likely threats to exploit known vulnerabilities

- Detect & Analysis – the organization detects a security incident and analyzes the impact

- Containment & Eradication – stop the security incident

- Post-incident Activities – learn from the incident and take action to prevent it from happening or be prepared if it happens again

Copyright © 2022 by Bruce Brown

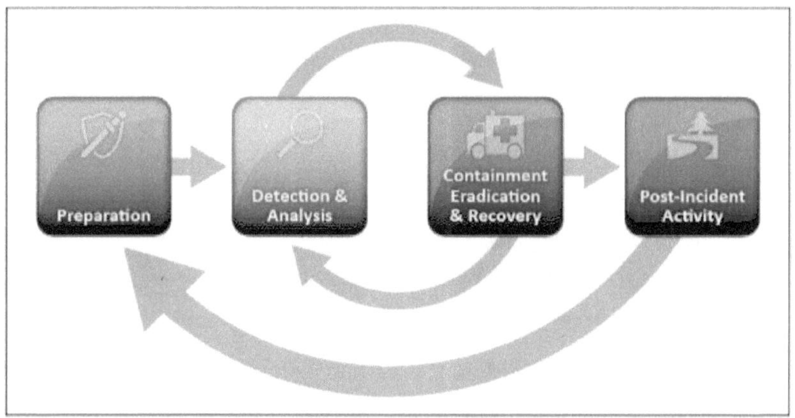

Incident Response Process – DHS.gov

Controls that are most helpful to the SCA include (but are not limited to):

- IR-1, Policy and Procedures
- IR-2, Incident Response Training
- IR-4, Incident Handling
- IR-5, Incident Monitoring
- IR-6, Incident Reporting
- IR-8, Incident Response Plan

Examination of the IR – Incident Response Controls

The incident response process should be well documented. The evidence should point to an active incident response process. These documents will show an overall policy or plan for the IR activities and detailed guides or procedures explaining how to handle certain incidents. Here are some examples of what the assessor can observe:

- Incident response policy or plan – IR policy or plans will be documents that are high-level, so they won't have many details and will be written for a large audience. This document will state the organization's need for incident response, what incidents are covered, and who is affected. The assessor is

Copyright © 2022 by Bruce Brown

looking for these documents to be reviewed regularly. Sometimes IR is mentioned in other documents, such as a security policy.

- Incident response procedures – IR procedures are a step-by-step guide on what users and stakeholders do during a security incident. This may include how to activate an incident response team. There may be an incident response procedure for each type of incident.

- Evidence of Incident response training – An after-action report (AAR), minutes, or notes are a way to verify if training is happening to prepare for incidents. The SCA checks to see if the incident procedures are used and if the policy is followed.

- Evidence of actual Incident response (tickets, reports, emails) – A security incident has recently happened in some cases. If the organization used the procedures and followed the IR policy, the assessor can use the evidence from the incident to show compliance. Evidence of the incident could include:

  - Incident reports
  - Tickets generated in response to the incident
  - Emails showing the response to the incident

Interviewing for IR – Incident Response Controls

The assessor can sit with the security team and ask questions about the incident response progress to validate the controls. If the organization is practicing the IR process regularly, then the cybersecurity team will be able to answer these questions:

- Is there any documentation on incident response?

- When was the last time you had a security incident? What procedures were used?

- Is there an incident response team? Who is on it?

- Can I see your IR documentation?

Copyright © 2022 by Bruce Brown

- Do you have exercises for security incidents?
- How do you detect security incidents?

Testing the IR – Incident Response Controls

The assessor can have the stakeholders demonstrate if the organization has automated testing, incident reporting, or training. The demonstration will show a process at work and how it works. It's mostly high or moderate-impact systems that will have automation.

Automation:

IR-3(1), Incident Response testing – Automated testing, the organization uses an automated system to help test the effectiveness of the incident response.

IR-6(1), Incident reporting – automated reporting. Some security information event management systems (like LogRhythm and Splunk) can do automated incident responses and reporting.

No.	Control Name	Low-Impact	Moderate-Impact	High-Impact	Privacy Control Baseline
IR-1	POLICY AND PROCEDURES	IR-1	IR-1	IR-1	IR-1
IR-2	INCIDENT RESPONSE TRAINING	IR-2	IR-2	IR-2 (1) (2)	IR-2 (3)
IR-3	INCIDENT RESPONSE TESTING		IR-3 (2)	IR-3 (2)	IR-3
IR-4	INCIDENT HANDLING	IR-4	IR-4 (1)	IR-4 (1) (4) (11)	IR-4
IR-5	INCIDENT MONITORING	IR-5	IR-5	IR-5 (1)	IR-5
IR-6	INCIDENT REPORTING	IR-6	IR-6 (1) (3)	IR-6 (1) (3)	IR-6
IR-7	INCIDENT RESPONSE ASSISTANCE	IR-7	IR-7 (1)	IR-7 (1)	IR-7
IR-8	INCIDENT RESPONSE PLAN	IR-8	IR-8	IR-8	IR-8 (1)
IR-9	INFORMATION SPILLAGE RESPONSE				
IR-10	INTEGRATED INFORMATION SECURITY ANALYSIS TEAM				

IR Control Family

Red Flags of IR Controls

Most organizations take action when they have a security incident, but some don't have a comprehensive process for handling them. If they don't have an overall policy with processes that break down how

Copyright © 2022 by Bruce Brown

they deal with incidents, this might point to deficiencies in the IR and other controls.

Green Flags of IR controls

When an organization has had a security incident that they successfully handled and documented, this is great evidence of a robust IR process.

Incident Response (IR) Resources

- NIST 800-53
- NIST 800-81, Computer Security Incident Handling Guide

Copyright © 2022 by Bruce Brown

MA – Maintenance

Maintaining the systems and surrounding infrastructure housing the systems is important to the organization. This is where overall maintenance comes in. This included everything from heating and ventilation system checkups to vendor contracts. The SCA will validate if the organization is keeping up with maintenance.

The SCA must know that the organization regularly checks mission-critical and supporting systems.

MA – Maintenance controls include:

- Repairing & replacing legacy systems
- Monitoring maintenance alerts on systems
- Performing diagnostics
- Preventative maintenance

The most used and visible MA controls include:

- MA-1, Policy, and Procedures
- MA-2, Controlled Maintenance
- MA-3, Maintenance Tools

Examination of the MA – Maintenance Controls

The SCA must observe whether the vendor maintenance contracts of mission essential systems are current. Not all systems will have a vendor support agreement or maintenance contract, but the assessor needs to know what happens when the system breaks. Let's say the server that does their main business gets a power surge and kills the

Copyright © 2022 by Bruce Brown

power supply. There should be a documented process explaining the process of fixing that system. The assessor needs to see that.

And what about the surrounding systems that keep the mission going? The power, heating, and cooling. If the organization needs a power generator, the assessor can check the maintenance records to determine when the generator was serviced. The same applies to heating, ventilation, and air conditioning (HVAC) systems.

Systems that should be examined for maintenance controls:

- Generator maintenance logs
- HVAC maintenance logs
- Vendor support agreement
- Visitor logs showing vendor entry
- Maintenance contracts

The assessor is looking for logs, contracts, and agreements that cover the last year. This will show that the organization has ongoing maintenance. Some indications that maintenance is not at an acceptable level are:

- Systems that have not been serviced in 1 year
- HVAC with no maintenance in years
- Generator with no maintenance in years
- No maintenance contracts at all

Interview on the MA – Maintenance Controls

The facility manager or equivalent is one of the best people to talk to about the support systems, power supply, and environment housing the business and mission systems. These are the groundskeepers, custodians, site managers, or anyone responsible for ensuring HVAC systems are running, and generators are fueled up. The assessor must talk to the system, subject matter experts, or managers for system support.

Copyright © 2022 by Bruce Brown

Interview questions for maintenance of systems:

- Do you have a service contract for the system?
- Is the service contract current?
- When was the last time maintenance done on the system?
- What do you do when the system malfunctions?
- What is the process of getting maintenance people in secure areas?

Interview questions for facility managers:

- When was the last time the HVAC system was serviced?
- When was the last time the generator was serviced?
- Is there a contract for servicing the HVAC and generators?
- Do these systems have alerts if they go down?
- What happens if the power goes out?
- What does the organization do if the HVAC goes down?

**Note: this is an opportunity to ask some PE questions that cover environmental controls.*

With these questions, the assessor is trying to get an attestation (a statement from someone within the organization) that gives some idea of how effective maintenance is.

Red Flags of MA Controls

Some telltale signs that their MA controls are lacking are no maintenance logs. Support systems such as HVAC and generators (if applicable) should have some sort of manual or automatic accounting of when the system was serviced. Some sites will not have any of this. Not have up to date contracts, and agreements are common to find in assessments.

Copyright © 2022 by Bruce Brown

Green Flags of MA Controls

As an assessor, whenever I could talk to a facility manager about the maintenance at the site, it went well. Cybersecurity, system administrators, and compliance officers don't usually know the ongoing maintenance of support systems like HVAC or generators. The facility managers are setting up the maintenance, so they know what's happening.

Maintenance Resources

- NIST 800-88, Guide for Media Sanitation

- NIST 140-3, Security Requirements for Cryptographic Modules

- Vendor end-of-life data

Copyright © 2022 by Bruce Brown

MP – Media Protection Control Assessment

The MP and Media Protection controls will be assessed through examination and interviews. Media generated by the organization includes (but is not limited to):

- Drives
- Printouts
- flash drives
- discs
- publications

Media is anything outside of a computer system that contains information. The assessor will determine whether or not the media is protected.

Protection of media generated by the organization means covering and labeling printouts with classifications.

The organization must have a process of properly marking, storing, transporting, sanitizing, and using digital and non-digital media.

Observing the top MP controls will show the assessor a lot:

- MP-1, Policy, and Procedures
- MP-2, Media Access – controlling access to digital and non-digital media.
- MP-3, Media Marking – marking the proper classification of digital and non-digital media.

Copyright © 2022 by Bruce Brown

Examination of MP – Media Protection Controls

An assessor can observe drives, documents, discs, and other media left out I the facility.

If the assessor can walk around the facility, they will pay close attention to any loose documents on desks and printers. They are looking for important information on those documents. If the documents contain classified data, personally identifiable information, or any important information, they should be labeled, covered, or put away somewhere safe. The assessor really should not see the information on classified documents. If they do, this should be documented because it may violate MP controls.

If the organization allows flash drives, they should be labeled.

Interview for the MP – Media Protection Controls

Since most of the organization's process of protecting media will not be observable from one short visit, an interview will be able to tell the assessor much more.

They must ask how the organization transports, sanitizes, labels, and covers its digital and non-digital media.

- How do you protect sensitive documents? Are disks flash drives?

- What are the classifications of data that you have here? How do you label the different classifications of information?

- Is there a policy or procedure for sensitive documents that are left out?

- If flash drives are allowed, how are they labeled?

- Where are disks, drives, and documents with sensitive information stored?

- How are sensitive documents transported from one site to another?

Copyright © 2022 by Bruce Brown

- How are sensitive documents destroyed once they are no longer in use?

- How are hard drives and flash drives erased or sanitized for reuse?

Assessors are trying to determine whether the organization's media protection process is thorough enough to protect the level of sensitivity that the information has. For a nonprofit organization that develops and maintains websites with publicly available information, they won't need to worry as much about sensitive information being left on a reception desk. But a missile defense unit under the United States Air Force, with many types of classified data, will need a robust program to protect all media types. The more types of media they allow, the greater the likelihood of exposure.

Red Flags of MP Controls

If you walk around the facility and see classified documents lying around with no covers and no protection, this could indicate a lack of MP controls. Some organizations have no process for protecting media with sensitive data.

Green Flags of Access Management

Having a media protection policy and procedure that the organization follows goes much further than many organizations I have seen.

Copyright © 2022 by Bruce Brown

PE – Physical and Environmental Protection

If the physical controls are within the scope of the assessment, the SCA may need to walk around the inside and the outside of the area where the system is held. They need to document the physical protections of the system. There should be physical boundaries that protect the system. PE controls include physical restrictions and a stable environment allowing the system's essential functions to operate. These support systems provide electricity, temperature, and even humidity controls.

Examination of PE - Physical Access Control

The assessor needs to look at the physical control policy first. This will give direction on what physical and operational controls the organization says they have. Suppose there are no formally approved physical control plans or policies. In that case, the assessor can use directives and laws from parent organizations, governing federal departments, and applicable state, local or industry authorities. All of them will use best security practices.

The assessor can also look at process documents if there are no policies. Checklists and work instructions can help to establish what the organization has mandated. Use these resources to determine if proper security is in place.

The organization must be the ones to dictate what physical security is necessary because they are in the best position to identify their threats and weaknesses.

Copyright © 2022 by Bruce Brown

The documentation will tell the assessor if there is supposed to be things like a physical security unit checking all badges at a front desk, if there is supposed to be fencing around the area, or if there is an electronic badging process for all authorized employees. The primary controls that the policy covers are PE-2 and PE-3:

- PE-2, Physical Access Authorizations – Maintain a list of individuals authorized access to the facility where the system is.

- PE-3, Physical Access Control – Enforce physical access authorizations to the system.

The physical security measures should be at a level that matches the classification and importance of the information being stored, processed, and transmitted. The assessor is looking for these controls to be implemented with physical and operational security controls. Physical security is restricting or deterring access with barriers and force, while operational security includes the behaviors of workers and rules to protect the system.

Not all physical security boundaries listed below will be necessary at every place, but just keep in mind that whatever they say they have in the physical security documentation should be in place. And the more sensitive the information is, the more security controls you should see.

Physical controls observed:

- List of authorized personnel or electronic system that validates authorized each individual

- Entryways are secured

- Parking areas are controlled or monitored

- Entryways are monitored

- The security unit checks entryways

Copyright © 2022 by Bruce Brown

- Accessible windows have alarm systems (for high-impact systems)
- Windows can be secured
- Windows do not allow people to view sensitive information
- Fencing (for high-impact systems)
- Vehicle obstructions (bollards, rocks, etc.)
- Alarm systems & Motion detectors

Operational security practices observed:

- Authorized personnel has a method of identification.
    - badges displayed
    - Name tags
    - Uniforms
- Personnel are challenged before accessing secure areas
    - Electronic badging system
    - Personally identified with ID upon entry
    - Metal detector / pat down (if applicable)
    - Biometric system upon entry
    - PIN code for access
- Areas with mission-essential systems are monitored
    - 24-hour guard
    - Closed-circuit television (CCTV)
    - Video footage saved and reviewed
- Authorized personnel with operational training
    - Social engineering exercises
    - Authorized individuals challenge possible trespassers

Examination of PE - Environmental Controls

To assess the environmental controls, the assessor will examine the main systems that support the information system they are assessing. Systems that manage the environment are temperature, humidity,

Copyright © 2022 by Bruce Brown

water, and power systems. Every environment is different, and these are not the only types of systems that can be used but the main ones.

Temperature & Humidity

Extreme cold and heat can damage the information system. For this reason, the assessor will check the heating, ventilation, and air conditioning (HVAC) to see if the organization has one. The organization might not need to use all the features of the HVAC system depending on the environment:

- Observe whether the organization has an HVAC system that can cover the size of the system being assessed

- In very dry climates, determine if there are humidity controls

- Has the HVAC system been serviced regularly

- The HVAC in a secure room with limited access

- Check on the maintenance log for the HVAC system

Water Damage Protection

Water damage protection is for organizations that have facilities with many resources in one area, like server rooms, data centers, etc. Having a facility with water pipes going through the same room with the assets is common. This is for cooling, sinks, bathrooms, and fire suppression systems. These rooms should have an isolation valve or a master shutoff valve. An isolation valve will allow the water to be cut off in the event of a leak, and a master shutoff switch can turn off the systems before they are wet. I have also seen computer rooms with water leak detection devices.

The following PE controls cover environmental system controls:

- PE-14, Environmental Controls – Maintain temperature, humidity, pressure, and radiation of the area that the system sits in. If necessary, the room or facility might need monitors

Copyright © 2022 by Bruce Brown

and alarms to make sure the environment remains controlled (PE-14(1); PE-14(2)).

- ☀ PE-15, Water Damage Protection – Protection of the system from damage from leaks by providing a master shutoff.

No.	Control Name	Low-Impact	Moderate-Impact	High-Impact	Privacy Control Baseline
PE-1	POLICY AND PROCEDURES	PE-1	PE-1	PE-1	
PE-2	PHYSICAL ACCESS AUTHORIZATIONS	PE-2	PE-2	PE-2	
PE-3	PHYSICAL ACCESS CONTROL	PE-3	PE-3	PE-3 (1)	
PE-4	ACCESS CONTROL FOR TRANSMISSION		PE-4	PE-4	
PE-5	ACCESS CONTROL FOR OUTPUT DEVICES		PE-5	PE-5	
PE-6	MONITORING PHYSICAL ACCESS	PE-6	PE-6 (1)	PE-6 (1) (4)	
PE-7	VISITOR CONTROL				
PE-8	VISITOR ACCESS RECORDS	PE-8	PE-8	PE-8 (1)	PE-8 (3)
PE-9	POWER EQUIPMENT AND CABLING		PE-9	PE-9	
PE-10	EMERGENCY SHUTOFF		PE-10	PE-10	
PE-11	EMERGENCY POWER		PE-11	PE-11 (1)	
PE-12	EMERGENCY LIGHTING	PE-12	PE-12	PE-12	
PE-13	FIRE PROTECTION	PE-13	PE-13 (1)	PE-13 (1) (2)	
PE-14	ENVIRONMENTAL CONTROLS	PE-14	PE-14	PE-14	
PE-15	WATER DAMAGE PROTECTION	PE-15	PE-15	PE-15 (1)	

PE Control Family

Copyright © 2022 by Bruce Brown

Interview of PE - Physical Access and Environmental Controls

Interviews are great for helping to assess the operation and environmental security of a system. Since operational security focuses on what authorized personnel are supposed to do to protect physical security, the assessor should be able to ask just about anyone these questions. Everyone should understand the physical restrictions that affect how they access facilities and surrounding areas. The most knowledgeable people about physical and operation controls will be the security unit (if there is one). Environmental controls are something most people ignore until they need them. Facility managers are the best people to interview for environmental controls.

Physical and Operation Questions:

- How are authorized users able to access the facilities? Are electronic cards used?

- Is there are security unit on site?

- Are there security systems?

- Are there cameras on site?

- Are the cameras monitored?

- How long is the footage of the camera kept?

- Is there a docking area? How is it secured?

- Are personnel required to wear badges to show they are authorized in certain areas?

- Do windows and doors have alarm systems?

- How often are alarm systems checked?

- Has there ever been a physical security incident? How did the organization respond?

Copyright © 2022 by Bruce Brown

Environment Controls Questions:

- Is there a backup generator? Does it have a supply of fuel? How long does the generator last? Does the generator last long enough to sustain essential functions while they move to an alternate site if all power is out for longer than expected?

- Is there an HVAC system?

- Is the HVAC system protected? Who has access to the HVAC system?

- When was the last time the HVAC had maintenance?

- Is the system in an enclosed area that will allow temperature controls?

- When was the last time the generator was serviced?

- Is there an isolation valve or master shutoff switch in the server room?

- Is there training or instructions given on what to do in the event of potential fire or water damage?

- Are there alerts for water detection?

Many other questions can be asked of PE security, but the most important are the ones that verify what they say they are doing in their policy or in line with the basic security of their industry.

Testing of PE - Physical Access Control

Seeing the alarms, locks, and processes in action is the best way to test them. Assessors can get very creative with physical security. But they need to make sure someone in a position of authority knows that they will test the limits of physical security before they do it.

Here are some things assessors can do to test physical security:

- Try to go into random doors

- Attempt to just walk into secure areas with no badge or credentials

Copyright © 2022 by Bruce Brown

- Set off an alarm system

- Set up an unauthorized entry scenario by walking into a door that is not normally used for entry

- Show a fake ID to enter a secure facility (you need approval for this, I cannot stress this enough)

- Walk around the facility unannounced to see if you will be detected or challenged

Red Flags of PE Controls

A lack of PE controls will be apparent almost immediately on systems with a need for a high level of protection. As soon as you arrive on site, you will notice people with no badges displayed properly, no security unit, and no cameras, and you start to wonder how they even protect this system.

Green Flags of PE Controls

If there is a need for a 24/7 security unit, this mitigates a lot of risk for PE controls. When organizations can afford to hire a professional security service, they will identify and cover many risks.

PE – Physical and Environmental Protection Resources

FIPS 201-2, Personal Identity Verification (PIV) of Federal Employees and Contractors

- NIST SP 800-73-4, Interfaces for PIV Verification

- NIST SP 800-116, Guidelines for the Use of PIV Credentials in Facility Access

Copyright © 2022 by Bruce Brown

PL – Planning

Since PL controls deal with system security plans, privacy plans, rules of behavior, and other documents, the assessor can have the organization's POC send the appropriate files before they arrive.

The assessor will review these essential planning documents to help validate controls.

The most foundational PL controls include:

- PL-1, Policy and Procedures
- PL-2, System Security and Privacy Plan
- PL-3, Rules of Behavior

Examine the PL – Planning controls

One of the first things the assessor will ask for is the system security plan (SSP). This document summarizes all the security controls on a system. Having this document will make the entire assessment easier because they can use it to reference how the controls should be implemented. Before assessing the username and password setup, they can review the identification and authentication controls in the SSP to see how the organization says they have implemented the control.

In this way, they can cross reference every control within the scope of the security assessment plan to see if it has been documented, effectively implemented, or even applicable.

The system security plan might be named differently and comes in many formats. It can be a spreadsheet, a database, a content management system, a PDF, or a set of text documents. I have seen the system security plan called by the content management system

Copyright © 2022 by Bruce Brown

that manages it, like eMASS, Archer, or Xacta. Sometimes the organization calls it by a contract name like Cyber Security Assessment Management (CSAM) or Information Technology (IT) Security Risk Management. Regardless of the name, this data collection summarizes how each control is installed, configured, and set up. These are called "implementation statements." The assessor needs to look at statements on each security control identified in the security assessment plan.

Interview for the PL – Planning controls

One of the things I've had to do as an assessor is sit down with the cybersecurity professional assigned to the system and ask questions about certain parts of their system security plans and policies. I may need to double-check that I have the most updated document or ask why certain controls seem missing from what was provided. My PL questions center around the documentation provided; sometimes, I would review the document while they were there and ask questions as I went.

Questions to ask with PL controls:

- Are there relevant implementation statements that describe how the security control is implemented?

- Is there evidence of the implementation statements?

- Has the system security plan been updated in the last year?

- Does the system security plan have a description of the system being assessed?

- Does the system security plan reference other documents that explain what's going on for items with no implementation statement?

- What control family does the organization use?

Copyright © 2022 by Bruce Brown

While reviewing the system security plan, the SCA might also examine the system's concept of operation (CONOPS). This is a high-level description of "why" the system exists and the basic functions necessary to complete the main mission or goal of the system. The system security plan usually has this in the executive summary and description of the system being assessed. Additional documents may go into greater detail about the systems CONOPs. This is part of PL controls as well, but if you hit the system security plan, you hit this and other important PL controls.

Rules of Behavior

Rules of behavior are often documented in the organization's user agreement or human resources. The assessor can review these documents to determine if there are rules of behavior. These rules tell users what they can and cannot do while on the system being assessed. The users with access to the system must read, understand, and agree to the terms set forth by the organization.

The assessor can examine the following documents to evaluate the existence of rules of behavior (PL-4):

- User authorization agreement
- Human resources policy on users
- User orientation documentation
- User restriction on social media restrictions
- Signed acknowledgment
- Rules of behavior policy
- Security policy addressing rules of behavior

Red Flags of PL controls

I have been to places where there is no system security plan. They would throw something together that addresses overall security but would have no breakdown of all the controls. If they don't have

Copyright © 2022 by Bruce Brown

something documenting the security controls, how thorough are they, especially in medium and large environments?

Green Flags of PL controls

It's always good when the assessor can get their hands on the most current system security plan of the system being assessed. It gives them an idea of the system's scope, functionality, and security layout. It will help them assess controls.

Copyright © 2022 by Bruce Brown

PM – Program Management Assessment

Program management (PM) controls address how the organization handles information security and risk. Since assessments are usually done on controls on a specific system, these controls are usually not applicable. However, if PM controls are implemented, this will let assessors know the organization has security processes in place that covers the system being assessed. For example, PM-9 covers the organization's risk management strategy. The assessor might be able to use any risk management strategy to determine if the system has a process of dealing with security incidents and vulnerabilities (IR and SI controls).

Examine the PM – Program Management controls

PM controls focus on how the organization manages risk, but some documentation can help when conducting the assessment.

Information security and privacy resources (PM-3)

This control focuses on the organizations funding for the security and privacy of systems. The assessor could use the documentation produced for PM-3 to help assess the "allocation of resources" (SA-2) needed. The system must have funding and planning for privacy and security.

Plan of Action and Milestone process (PM-4)

PM-4 is a control that ensures the organization has a plan of action and milestone (POA&M) process for all systems. If a system control is missing, a POA&M is one of the documents that an assessor will

Copyright © 2022 by Bruce Brown

expect to see. If the organization has this process in place, this helps a lot.

System Inventory (PM-5)

System inventory is crucial to baseline, configuration (CM), and other controls. If the assessor can examine, test, or ask questions about the organization's system inventory, this can cover more than one control. Validation of a system inventory covers AC-3, CM-8, PL-8, and many other controls.

Enterprise Architecture (PM-7)

PM-7 is a control that ensures the organization includes privacy and security features when the system is developed and maintained. If this is being done, the assessor will see minutes from the change management or configuration meetings that include the cybersecurity team. The assessor will see audit logs turned on and used on the system and security software like malware protection tools.

Risk Management Strategy (PM-9)

This control covers the organization's process of dealing with risks. The assessor should see a strategy to manage risks to the organization's operations, systems, and individuals. This is very broad, but specific things this will produce include (but are not limited to):

- Threat hunting
- Security operations center
- Vulnerability management
- Incident response reports

Copyright © 2022 by Bruce Brown

Authorization Process (PM-10)

The assessor can look at any updated and management-approved document explaining the system authorization process. These documents may help to validate the control CA-6, Authorization. This document will show things like the assigned authorizing official, the authorized official for common controls, and the authorization process itself.

No.	Control Name	Low-Impact	Moderate-Impact	High-Impact	Privacy Control Baseline
PM-1	INFORMATION SECURITY PROGRAM PLAN				
PM-2	INFORMATION SECURITY PROGRAM LEADERSHIP ROLE				
PM-3	INFORMATION SECURITY AND PRIVACY RESOURCES				PM-3
PM-4	PLAN OF ACTION AND MILESTONES PROCESS				PM-4
PM-5	SYSTEM INVENTORY				PM-5 (1)
PM-6	MEASURES OF PERFORMANCE				PM-6
PM-7	ENTERPRISE ARCHITECTURE				PM-7
PM-8	CRITICAL INFRASTRUCTURE PLAN				PM-8
PM-9	RISK MANAGEMENT STRATEGY				PM-9
PM-10	AUTHORIZATION PROCESS				PM-10
PM-11	MISSION AND BUSINESS PROCESS DEFINITION				PM-11
PM-12	INSIDER THREAT PROGRAM				
PM-13	SECURITY AND PRIVACY WORKFORCE				PM-13

Red Flags of PM Controls

PM controls are about how the organization handles its overall information security program. It is not system specific, but if the organization seems to be all over the place with its information system security strategy, this may adversely affect the security posture of the system being assessed.

Copyright © 2022 by Bruce Brown

Green Flags of PM Controls

When the organization has a solid information system security program, risk strategy, and system inventory, this helps keep all systems in line. It's really about how much of their strategy they implement.

Copyright © 2022 by Bruce Brown

PS – Personnel Security Assessment

The assessor starts evaluating the PS controls, and personnel security, as soon as the process of getting on the site starts.

PS controls are assessed for how the organization handles personnel who can enter facilities, come near resources, and interact with essential mission employees. The assessor makes sure the organization thoroughly vets everyone that is allowed entry and determines the level of access they have. The organization should assign a level of risk to each position and then screen them based on that position. For example, a person with a janitorial position should have a different screening level than a senior executive analyst whose position requires access to classified material. Both positions require some screening, but the position with the higher level of access will require much more.

The most used and visible PS controls include:

- PS-1, Policy, and Procedures
- PS-3, Personnel Screening
- PS-4, Personnel Termination
- PS-6, Access Agreements

Examine the PS – Personnel Security controls

The assessor should note how the organization screens them to gain temporary site and resource access. If there is no process to vet an outside assessor, this is a red flag. This will prompt the assessor to look deeper into the documented personnel security process.

Copyright © 2022 by Bruce Brown

Along with observing the process as they are going through the process, here are some personnel security documents that the assessor can examine:

- Personnel security plan
- Human resources documents on orientation and screening
- Policy and procedures for screening
- System security plan
- Procedures addressing position categorization
- List of risk designations for positions
- Observe position descriptions

Interview for the PS – Personnel Security controls

If there is no process to vet an outside assessor, the assessor should ask why there is no personnel security process. Assessors normally interview a subject matter expert on personnel security. This could be the cybersecurity representative, personnel screener, human resources, security manager, or any authorized person who knows the personnel security process of the organization.

- What is the screening process for new personnel?
- Are different levels of screening for different positions? (Such as background checks)
- What is the process for employees and contractors who leave?
- Is there a process for personnel being transferred?

The assessor is looking for attestation that there is a screening process that looks at different positions.

Red Flags of Access Management

As the assessor, if I can walk right into an organization with little or no checks of who I am and no pre-authorization, that is a red flag. Getting authorization to assess the system is a pain, but it is necessary.

Copyright © 2022 by Bruce Brown

Green Flags of Access Management

If the organization is strict and thorough with the assessors, there is a good chance they are like this with every new organization that needs access to mission essential assets. Being escorted everywhere with a temporary badge is a good sign.

No.	Control Name	Low-Impact	Moderate-Impact	High-Impact	Privacy Control Baseline
PS-1	POLICY AND PROCEDURES	PS-1	PS-1	PS-1	
PS-2	POSITION RISK DESIGNATION	PS-2	PS-2	PS-2	
PS-3	PERSONNEL SCREENING	PS-3	PS-3	PS-3	
PS-4	PERSONNEL TERMINATION	PS-4	PS-4	PS-4 (2)	
PS-5	PERSONNEL TRANSFER	PS-5	PS-5	PS-5	
PS-6	ACCESS AGREEMENTS	PS-6	PS-6	PS-6	PS-6
PS-7	EXTERNAL PERSONNEL SECURITY	PS-7	PS-7	PS-7	
PS-8	PERSONNEL SANCTIONS	PS-8	PS-8	PS-8	
PS-9	POSITION DESCRIPTIONS	PS-9	PS-9	PS-9	

Copyright © 2022 by Bruce Brown

PT – Personally Identifiable Information (PII) Processing and Transparency Assessment

As assessors, we must see personally identifiable information (PII) as sensitive information (because it is). As such, the organization should be identifying and protecting it. As a part of the assessment, the assessor will be looking for not only reviewing network security results, operation security, and access controls but protection of PII. PII is always within the scope of every assessment.

For example, let's say the assessor is only supposed to examine the system security plan to ensure it is approved, complete, and current. This might sound like it has nothing to do with PII. If, for whatever reason, the system security plan has full names associated with dates of birth, home addresses and phone numbers of contractors, and other unnecessary PII information, the assessor should call this out. They should point this out just like they would if they saw classified information or exposed passwords in the vulnerability scan. The assessor is looking for the organization to identify which systems have PII and protection of systems with lots of sensitive PII such as social security numbers and medical records. If websites are within the scope of the assessment, the assessor may need to see if the organization is allowing users to consent to collections of PII.

The assessor is also looking for whether the organization has a process for protecting PII and remaining compliant with federal regulations.

Copyright © 2022 by Bruce Brown

Examination of PT – Personally Identifiable Information (PII) controls

While observing documentation and systems, the assessor should watch for employee and customer information. If they see it, they should determine if it is protected rather than publicly available or displayed in common areas for all to see. Full names, work emails, and work phone numbers are expected, but the assessor will note PII that can be linked together to exploit an individual.

We mentioned the full name and work emails, but if this information also contains personal addresses, place of birth, or financial information, this could be used to exploit an individual. The assessor must observe whether this PII is necessary for the document and whether it is properly protected.

The assessor is looking for the following PII:

- Full name
- Personal Telephone number
- Personal address
- Social security numbers
- Passport number
- Driver's license
- Biometric data
- Date of Birth
- Place of birth
- Business phone number
- Employment information
- Credit card number
- Financial account number
- Medical records

Copyright © 2022 by Bruce Brown

An assessor will need to observe the following documents to go deeper into the system's adherence to PII protection:

- Privacy impact assessment (policy, procedures, or results)
- Privacy threshold analysis (policy, procedures, or results)
- System of Records Notices (SORN), if applicable
- System security or privacy plan
- Security or privacy policy
- Privacy policy (for web applications)

Please note that privacy assessments are only necessary if the organization has PII being processed, transmitted, or stored on the system being assessed. A system of records notice is only for federal systems that maintain a searchable system of records.

Interviewing for PT – Personally Identifiable Information (PII) controls

The assessor needs to interview someone who knows what PII is, the PII protection process, knows what a privacy assessment is, and is familiar with security compliance. This would normally be an information system security officer, someone in a compliance position, a privacy officer, a cybersecurity professional, or a system administrator familiar with the privacy policies. Most people are just not aware of the organization's PII processes.

There are technical and process questions that will cover most of the NIST 800 PT controls:

- PT-1, Policy and Procedures
- PT-3, PII processing purpose
- PT-4, Consent
- PT-6, System of Records Notice

Copyright © 2022 by Bruce Brown

Technical PT questions:

- Does the web page of the system have a privacy statement?
- Is the privacy statement visible to users?
- How does the web page give consent to use PII?
- Does the site use cookies that collect information from users?
- What is used to protect PII on the system?
- Does the organization have systems of records that include PII?

Please note that these technical questions are only necessary if the system being assessed has a web page or a system that collects PII from visitors; this may include cookies.

Operational & Management PT questions:

- Does the organization address PII and privacy in its policy?
- Does the system collect PII?
- Has the system had a privacy impact assessment (RA-8)?
- Why is PII being processed, stored, or transmitted on the system being assessed?
- How is PII protected on the system being assessed?

Testing PT – Personally Identifiable Information (PII) controls

If the system being assessed has a web page or content management system that collects or tracks PII, the assessor needs to test the behavior of the system for the following:

Privacy policy

Consent

Privacy Transparency

Copyright © 2022 by Bruce Brown

The Privacy Policy

The assessor should ensure that the privacy policy is accessible on the site. This can be a pop-up or located somewhere in the page's header, body, or footer as soon as a user accesses the site. This policy provides the user with information about how the organization collects and uses information. This information should be in line with the organization's privacy policy.

Consent

To check for consent, the assessor can access the site of the system being assessed. Once on the site, the system should notify the user that their information is being collected or tracked if they go further. This is usually a pop-up on the main page with a button that allows the user to exit or go into the site.

Privacy Transparency

For federal systems to collect public information, site users must be informed of what the organization is doing with their PII. They should know that it is protected. The assessor will see this explained on the main site of the system being assessed.

Testing the pop-ups and consent on a system is only necessary for systems with a website that collects PII.

These controls ensure the user knows that the system is processing, storing, or transmitting their PII. PT controls are about letting users know what is being collected, why it is being collected, and giving consent.

Copyright © 2022 by Bruce Brown

No.	Control Name	Low-Impact	Moderate-Impact	High-Impact	Privacy Control Baseline
PT-1	POLICY AND PROCEDURES				PT-1
PT-2	AUTHORITY TO PROCESS PERSONALLY IDENTIFIABLE INFORMATION				PT-2
PT-3	PERSONALLY IDENTIFIABLE INFORMATION PROCESSING PURPOSES				PT-3
PT-4	CONSENT				PT-4
PT-5	PRIVACY NOTICE				PT-5 (2)
PT-6	SYSTEM OF RECORDS NOTICE				PT-6 (1) (2)
PT-7	SPECIFIC CATEGORIES OF PERSONALLY IDENTIFIABLE INFORMATION				PT-7 (1) (2)
PT-8	COMPUTER MATCHING REQUIREMENTS				PT-8

PT Controls Family

Red Flags of Access Management

Some organizations want to use social security numbers, DOB, and other unnecessary personal information. The military is notorious for this. The problem crops up protecting records after they have gathered all that PII.

Green Flags of Access Management

When an organization uses PII as little as possible, it shows that they are thinking ahead. They know they must protect all that personal data, so they don't use social security number if they must, they only use part of it.

Copyright © 2022 by Bruce Brown

Resources for PT, PII Controls

- Examples: https://www.ftc.gov/policy-notices/privacy-policy/privacy-impact-assessments

- https://www2.ed.gov/notices/ed-pia.html

- NIST 800-122, Guide to Protecting the Confidentiality of PII

- EPA: https://www.epa.gov/privacy/privacy-act-laws-policies-and-resources

    - Privacy Act of 1974

Copyright © 2022 by Bruce Brown

RA – Risk Assessment

Is the organization doing continuous monitoring by checking vulnerabilities, conducting network scans, and doing documentation based on risks that they find? SCAs are looking for this when looking into the RA control family. The organization should have a policy addressing how often scans are done on the assessed system. The cover is a control family that addresses all aspects of risk assessment. The tools for risk assessment, such as vulnerability scanners, come to mind, but this family covers security categorization, risk response, privacy impact assessments, and threat hunting.

The most used and visible RA controls include:

- RA-1, Policy and Procedures
- RA-2, Security Categorization
- RA-3, Risk Assessment
- RA-5, Vulnerability Monitoring, and Scanning
- RA-7, Risk Response

Examine the RA – Risk Assessment Controls

The assessor will look at the security policy to determine if the organization has documented to need for regular risk assessments, the frequency of the risk assessments, and what is covered in those assessments.

Once the assessor knows what is supposed to happen, they can look at what is happening. The evidence of risk assessments can be found in the following documents:

Copyright © 2022 by Bruce Brown

- Current and risk assessments reports

- System security plans

- Vulnerability scan schedules

- Privacy impact assessment results (if any)

The system security plan will also show whether assessments are being done. A regularly maintained system security plan will show updated implementation statements, updated documents, modification dates within the last year, and other evidence of continuously monitored controls. The assessed system should have a security categorization of Low, Moderate, or High (usually written in the security documentation itself.

For RA controls, the assessor is looking for whether assessments are being done internally or externally; the accuracy of the data is more important with SC and SI control than you are looking at the installation of security features.

Interviewing for RA – Risk Assessment Controls

As mentioned above, RA controls are mostly about the process, not the tools. When assessing an organization's process, interviews are often the best ways to determine what is being done and whether the key players know what is supposed to be done.

If the SCA has reviewed the policy, they will have some idea of the organization's risk assessment process. If the interview is still necessary, it will be enough to see if they are doing what they say in the documentation.

Here are some questions to ask that will help determine whether the RA process matches the RA controls:

- When was the last time a risk assessment was done?

- What is the current security categorization of systems?

- What vulnerability scanning tool is used, and how often?

Copyright © 2022 by Bruce Brown

- How often are network scans conducted?
- After scans are done, who reviews them?
- What is done if vulnerabilities are found?
- Who conducts the network and vulnerability scans?
- Who conducts the privacy impact assessments?
- Is there a security operations center? Is Threat hunting conducted?

Testing RA – Risk Assessment Controls

If the organization uses mechanisms to conduct assessments, the SCA can test these systems. Usually, assessors will have a subject matter expert get on the system and have them perform some activity that will allow them to observe the outcome. Systems that might perform risk assessments include (but are not limited to):

- Content management systems that allow risk assessments of documents
- Network & vulnerability scanners
- Security compliance scanners
- Wireless scanners
- Phishing campaign software

The tools of risk assessments should not be confused with the process and activity itself. I mean that risk assessments are not just using the Nessus scanner. It includes knowing what the assets are, analyzing the vulnerabilities of those assets, and identifying the likelihood of attack from threats. The assessor will determine if the organization is doing this regularly, but it is a huge plus that the SCA has been tasked with being a part of the risk assessment process.

Copyright © 2022 by Bruce Brown

Red Flags of RA Controls

RA is risk assessments, vulnerability monitoring and scanning, risk responses, and other data analysis methods. Most organizations do some form of risk assessment and self-analysis. The problems come when they don't conduct risk assessments regularly.

Green Flags of RA Controls

An organization with multiple ways of determining the risk of all aspects of its system is awesome! They have scans on their web applications and penetration testing on their external and DMZ. They have internal scans regularly. And a great risk assessment program even includes physical and policy checks.

Copyright © 2022 by Bruce Brown

SA – System and Services Acquisition

The best way for the assessor to approach the SA controls is to break them into three main topics: acquisitions, system, and software engineering. The assessor looks at how the organization purchases equipment and funds services for acquisitions. Assessors look at the process used for software development and system engineering for SA controls.

Examination of the SA Controls

The assessor must examine three areas to get a picture of the SA controls.

- System engineering documents
- System acquisitions and services
- Software development

Not all of these will apply to every system being assessed. For example, if there is no software development on the assessed system, this part of the SA control family will not apply.

Examination of System engineering documents

For system engineering, the assessor will look at whether the system has gone through a formal system development process. A formal process usually produces engineering documentation, meeting minutes, and diagrams. A good system development process will include security being considered early in development. Even with the systems that have been up for years, there should be engineering documents and meetings that have taken place recently with modifications and updates.

Copyright © 2022 by Bruce Brown

The documents that the assessor can look at include the following:

- System engineering concept of operations
- System development life cycle plans, process, and policy
- Network diagrams
- Engineering schematics
- Flow charts
- Minutes from change management
- Minutes for configuration management

Any documents that show that comprehensive technical and security planning took place during implementation and updates of the system being assessed.

The security controls that are pivotal to the assessment include:

- SA-3, System Development Life Cycle, means using the standard system engineering development life cycle.
- SA-8, Security and Privacy Engineering Principle, apply security controls throughout the engineering process
- SA-5, System documentation, involves creating and maintaining engineering documentation for the system.

Examination of Software Engineering

The assessor will need to look at the organization's software engineering process for systems with in-house software development. A couple of the more important controls for this are:

- SA-10, Developer Configuration Management - ensuring that the code and the systems that it is developed go through a configuration management process.
- SA-11, Developer Testing and Evaluation - testing the code to ensure all security and privacy controls are implemented correctly.

Copyright © 2022 by Bruce Brown

The software libraries used to write the code need to be protected. Only those with a need should be able to access these critical files. Any major changes in the software being developed must go through a configuration management process that will include all the main stakeholders, including an information security representative and the system owner. The changes and meetings should be documented. If major changes to the software can be made with no oversight and no documentation, this is a huge red flag that violates several security controls, including SA-10.

Testing should be conducted to evaluate the code before it is put into production.

Examination of the software engineering process can be done by looking at the following:

- Software change configurations meeting notes
- Software development policy
- Software development process
- Results of the software development tests
- Evidence of a secure software library

The most used and visible SA controls include:

- SA-1, Policy, and Procedures
- SA-3, System Development Life Cycle
- SA-4, Acquisition Process
- SA10, Developer Configuration Management

Examination of System Acquisitions and Services

The assessor needs to see if the organization buys equipment and services securely.

The organization should follow an acquisition process (SA-4, acquisition process) to purchase equipment and services for the system being assessed.

Copyright © 2022 by Bruce Brown

The analyzed documentation will not always be with the information security documentation (such as a paragraph in the security policy). Many organizations have a separate department that handles all contracts, agreements, and acquisitions. The documents that the assessor can check out include the following:

- Contracts necessary for the information system being assessed
- Acquisition policy and procedures
- Organizational agreements

The assessor is trying to see if the organization has an acquisition process (some don't) and if current contracts can be renewed for the assessed system. They also want to ensure the organization is not buying mission-critical services and parts from unreliable sources.

Copyright © 2022 by Bruce Brown

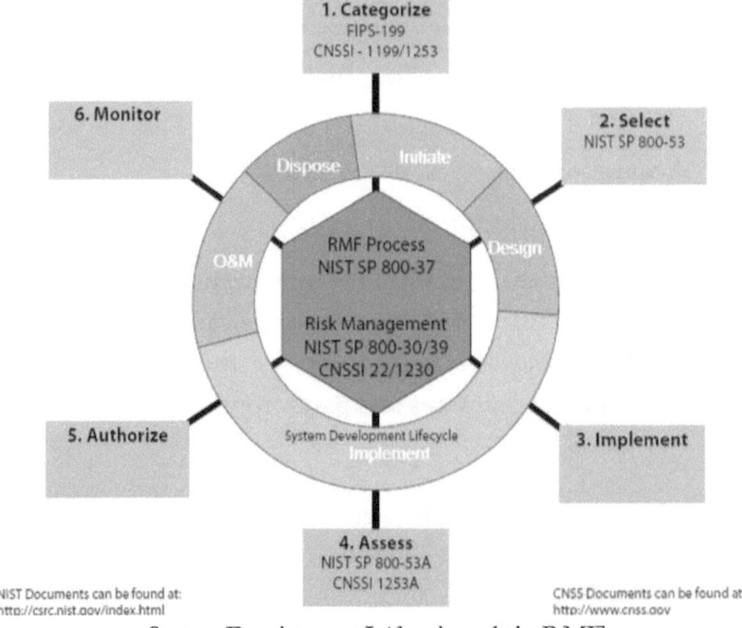

System Development Lifecycle and the RMF

Interviews on SA – System and Services Acquisition

The questions for SA – system and services acquisition vary because this is a broad family of controls. The stakeholders will also depend on whether the assessor deals with software development, acquisitions, or system engineering.

Interviewing for the Software development process

For software development, the assessor needs to talk to information system security personnel familiar with the protection and processes of software engineering. Software engineers and managers will be great resources for the assessor. The questions include:

Copyright © 2022 by Bruce Brown

- Does the software development include change management?
- Does software development have a configuration management process?
- What is the software development process?
- How are the software libraries protected?
- Is there a software engineering policy?

Interviewing for the System Engineering process

Managers, information security officers, and system engineers will have some of the best stakeholders to ask about this part of the SA controls. The questions focus on the organization's engineering processes. The assessor needs to validate if the security is part of the system engineering process:

- Did the system have a system engineering process?
- (For new systems) Are there security and privacy controls designed in the system?
- How are security and privacy controls considered when there are major changes in the system? Are they discussed in configuration management meetings?
- Are there any system engineering documents?

Interviewing for the Acquisition process

Information system security officers, compliance experts, and managers will have some idea of the acquisition process. And if they don't, they will know whom to talk to. If the organization has an acquisitions office, these are the people to talk to. The questions include:

- What is the acquisition process?
- How does the organization purchase new parts for the systems?

Copyright © 2022 by Bruce Brown

- Are there any services for the system? Examples: cloud, cybersecurity, Internet connectivity, services necessary for the essential functions of the system?

- Is the maintenance contract up to date?

Red Flags of SA Controls

If a system has software development, a lot of times, the related SA controls are neglected. The software developers themselves either don't know or don't care about the security controls and configuration process that is supposed to be done. So, this is an area where the assessor should investigate if applicable.

Green Flags of SA Controls

When organizations have managers who used to be system or software engineers, they usually have been around long enough to understand why security should be implemented early in the process. They are a great resource if the assessor can get them into an interview.

Copyright © 2022 by Bruce Brown

SC – System and Communications Protection

Assessment of SC controls is what most people think about when they think of assessments. The SC family is "system and communications protection." Assessments for these controls usually include network, endpoint, and server scanning. But SC control assessments are more than just scanning. They can also observe the audit logs and examine the policy, process, and procedures. They may need to test internal, external, and DMZ network access to detect vulnerabilities.

There are so many SC controls covering so many aspects of the organization's enterprise. The assessor needs to remain within scope. When acting in the SCA role, ensure you have target IP addresses or hostnames and stay within those systems. The organization will have issues introducing weaknesses outside the security assessment plan.

At the time of this writing, there are over 50 SC controls. Rather than focusing on each control and control enhancement (that may not even apply to the system being assessed), the SCA focuses on the objects being assessed to determine if the system is being protected. One simple way to breakdown the assessment of the SC controls is to categorize the types of assets they affect:

- Servers – servers have centralized functionality that multiple users use. The assessor is looking for weaknesses and exposure to threats to the server's functionality.

- Endpoint devices – Endpoint devices refer to laptops, desktops, notepads, and other devices that users use to do daily tasks. If not configured correctly, these systems can become the biggest entry point for malicious attackers.

Copyright © 2022 by Bruce Brown

- The network – The network's infrastructure comprises internetworking devices (switches and routers). The way the network is set up creates the system's boundary, which is one of the main focuses of the SC controls.

Other important objects and resources of the network are the people managing and using the network, peripheral devices, and artifacts that map out and document the network. Focusing on the servers, endpoints, and network keeps it simple.

Examination of SC controls for the Network

We will focus on the examination method, but the assessor will use a combination of observation, testing, and interviewing for all control families as big as the SC controls. For example, the assessor will examine the results of the vulnerability assessment report that came from testing. They may even ask questions while they are observing results.

If available, the assessor can look at the old assessment results to get an idea of where the problems were and the context (if it was documented). The network diagram will show the components used and how the network is laid out.

The documentation will give some idea of best security practices across the network. Some of the basic things include:

- Encryption of critical data
- Update of network software (network devices, antimalware software)
- Access controls by the security policies
- Event logs being collected
- Update of the network documentation
- Education of network users
- Multiple layers of defense

Copyright © 2022 by Bruce Brown

- Control of ports, protocols, and services across the network

The documentation will give the assessor an idea of their adherence to security controls.

The documents that the assessor can look at include the following:

- Network diagrams

- Old network scans

- Network engineering documents

- Security policy addressing network standards

- Ports, protocols, and services lists

- SC controls addressed in System security plans

- Privacy impact assessments

- Engineering documents that address encryption

- Processes and procedures addressing networking

- Security training on network usage

The assessor is looking at the content of the documents to verify that security best practices are being met. These best practices link to security controls. It's important that the artifacts are up to date and authorized by up-level management.

Some critical network security controls are addressed in the SC family. These include encryption, planning against denial-of-service attacks, boundary protection, transmission integrity, and network-related security practices.

- SC-5, Denial of Service Protection, is a control that has the organization plan against denial-of-service attacks. An example might be increased network capacity or having the ability to quickly react and filter certain packets. This ensures that the system remains available.

Copyright © 2022 by Bruce Brown

- ❂ SC-7, Boundary Protection, manages and monitors the interfaces of gateways, routers, firewalls, guards, network-based malicious code, and other systems.

- ❂ SC-8 and SC-9, Transmission Confidentiality and Integrity, protect the confidentiality and integrity of data on internal and external networks as it travels from system to system.

Examination of SC controls for Server and Endpoint device components

SC controls deep dive into the settings and communication happening on servers and Endpoint devices in the environment. Assessment will happen on all types of servers, from virtual cloud bases images to big data clusters that are on-premises. The SCA will observe how the organization manages the security features of the individual systems within the assessment's scope.

SC-2 – Separation of System and User Function

The organization should be separating system and user functionality. This means that a standard user should be unable to control how the system collects logs or speed up the processor. These things are controlled by the system and configured by a privileged user when necessary. The system is locked down, so users cannot change it whenever they like it.

- ❂ SC-2, Separation of System and User Functionality – An example would be a computer with strict user roles that do not allow root or administrator access to the operating system. Most operating systems allow this, but extra settings need to be put in place to implement it.

Information in Shared System Resources

Many computers in large environments share multiple resources. For example, a desktop may have multiple employees login into the system to use the same hard drive. Modern systems use "profiles" so

Copyright © 2022 by Bruce Brown

that all users on the same system can use the same hard drive. The assessor needs to see that there are groups with different roles and permissions on the systems. This will show that the organization has some information protection on the shared systems.

- SC-4, Information in Shared System Resources, is to prevent the unauthorized transfer of shared information by creating groups with roles, creating permissions, and encrypting data.

The assessor looks at scan results, documentation, and processes during the observation process. The assessment starts broad, looking for basic things such as configuration management, access controls, identification and authentication, auditing, and many of the best security practices addressed in the other controls covering the assessed system. This might sound too obvious to mention, but you would be surprised how many organizations (important organizations like your bank, your hospital, and other institutions you trust with your information) do not do these basic things. Finding these gaps is what the assessment is for.

If you find these gaps as the assessor, you must look deeper into that area by observing more documentation, asking questions, and conducting tests.

We mentioned SC-2, the separation of user and system functions, and SC-4, information in shared system resources. However, there are many other best security practices that the SCA needs to look for during the assessment:

- Least functionality – Systems are only built with the capabilities necessary to do the work. (CM-7)

- Least privileges – Making sure that the system users have only enough privileges to do their work. (AC-6)

- Baseline Configuration – system adheres to configurations set by the organization. (CM-2)

Copyright © 2022 by Bruce Brown

- System backups – The system's important information is backed up (if necessary).

- Vulnerability management – the system's vulnerabilities are fixed in a time frame created by the organization. (SI-2)

- System support – end-of-life systems and applications are being replaced with supported versions, and applications with no vendor to support them are managed or excluded from the environment. (SA-22)

- Change controls – any system changes are managed with meetings, documentation such as tickets, and system impact analysis. (CM-3)

These are just some of the best security practices that an SCA can determine based on examining the processes and documents created for the system. You will notice that these all link back to other NIST 800 control families. During the server and Endpoint device assessment, that assessor determines if the security controls are technically implemented on the systems for the SC controls.

The documents that the assessor can review for the servers and Endpoint devices include the following:

- Baseline configuration policies, procedures, standards

- Group Policy Object (GPO) or any collection of system policy settings for operating systems

- Security policies addressing server and endpoint settings

- Work instructions for server and endpoint device setup

- Access control documentation

- Audit logs showing access restrictions on servers and Endpoint devices

Copyright © 2022 by Bruce Brown

Interview of SC controls for Network and Network components

An interview with network security starts with getting the right points of contact. Network engineering is highly specialized, and not all IT personnel will know how it works, let alone how it is laid out. The assessor needs to talk to network operators, network engineering, or IT people who are very familiar with the inner workings of the network.

- Are there network policies and procedures in place?

- Are there areas of the network that need to be separated from the rest of the production network? (Examples of this might be a test network or a classified management network)

- Is there an internal, external, and DMZ network? Is there a denial of services protection if there is an external network? (SC-5)(SC-7)

- Are there shares on the network? If so, how are they protected? (SC-4)

- Is the network monitored? If so, How? (SC-7)

Interview of SC controls for Servers and Endpoint devices

System administrators will be the servers' and Endpoint devices' best contact points. The SC controls have some information system-based questions that the typical network jockey won't know. Server and endpoint systems get very detailed.

- Does the organization have a policy or procedure that directs how the systems on the network will be configured? (SC-01)

- What types of groups and roles are on the servers and Endpoint devices? (SC-02)

- Do regular users have local administrator rights on their endpoint devices? (SC-02)

Copyright © 2022 by Bruce Brown

- Are their shared folders? Do user roles lock them down?

- Does the system have host-based protections? (SC-7)

- Are communications monitored on endpoints and servers (SC-7)?

- Does the organization isolate mission-essential systems? (SC-7(21))

- How is personally identifiable information protected in the system? (SC-7(24)

- How are systems with classified information protected? (SC-7(24)) (SC-7(26))

Testing of SC controls

The SCA needs to be well-versed in scanning tools and techniques to run tests on an organization's network. Before anything is done, they need written permission that includes the scope of what will be scanned, the type of testing or assessment, when it will be conducted, and who is conducting the test. There are many types of network tests, including:

- Internal network scans

- System compliance scan

- Security policy platforms

- External network scans

- DMZ scans

- Penetration testing

- Web application scans

- Wireless scans

- Firewall scanners

What all these network scans have in common is that they typically consist of a range of systems (IP addresses) that must be

Copyright © 2022 by Bruce Brown

discovered", and "fingerprinted" before they are tested. These scans can be intrusive and can disrupt mission and business if performed at the wrong time. That's why it is very important that the scope is clearly defined and the SCA conducts the network test at the right time.

Credentialed vs. Noncredentialled Scans

A credentialed scan uses identification and authentication to log in to systems. For example, the scan will need to have a username and password so that it can run successfully. All of this must be done before the scan starts. During the planning phase, the SCA must ensure the proper credentials are set up. These credentials may require privileged access to see all vulnerabilities, patches, user rights, system settings, and configurations that a standard user account cannot access. The assessor must ensure these work before the official assessment starts because it sucks when this doesn't work and you only have one hour scheduled to run the scan on a critical system. Credentialed scans are usually done on internal, DMZ, endpoint, and compliance scans. "Blue Teams" or cybersecurity network defenders use credentialed scans to get a comprehensive view of all weaknesses that can be exploited. Information system security officers, governance, compliance, and risk professionals find credentialed scans useful to show where the organization complies with federal, state, or industry regulations.

Non-credentialed scans do not require identification and authentication to run. They only require a scope of IP addresses or hostnames and written permission to run at a certain date and time. These are usually used to look for what is exposed to unauthorized users and attackers. These are used for external and web app scans and penetration tests. "Red Teams," black hats, and hackers use these types of scans to gather information about a network to develop more sophisticated attacks.

Copyright © 2022 by Bruce Brown

Depending on the security assessment plan, the SCA will use a combination of these scans. One of the tricky things that the assessor should look out for is failed scans. They will need someone well-versed in the network scan being used to determine if the scan was successfully run.

The Scan Results

At the time of this writing, some of the popular scanning tools include Tenable, Qualys, Rapid7, and others. These vendors change as the market evolves and technology moves forward. By the time you read this, there will be many others. Most network scanners use a proprietary method of measuring risks on devices discovered on the network. The severity of the weaknesses is given a category:

- Informational (or none)
- Low
- Medium
- High
- Critical

These proprietary vulnerabilities use the Common Vulnerabilities and Exposures (CVE) system. CVE identifies each vulnerability. Since most scanners use these "Common Vulnerabilities" to map what they find, it allows cybersecurity professionals to know the level of risk. These CVEs are listed in the National Institute of Standards and Technology (NIST) National Vulnerability Database.

The CVEs use the Common Vulnerability Scoring System (CVSS) to rate the weakness identified. The CVSS identifies characteristics of each weakness to give them a final grade of severity. The severity tells us how it would be to exploit the weakness of a system.

Copyright © 2022 by Bruce Brown

A CVSS score ranges from 0.0 and 10.0, with 10.0 being the most severe. These numbers map to a certain severity category from none to critical:

- 0 = None.
- to 3.9 = Low
- to 6.9 = Medium
- to 8.9 = High
- 9.0 to 10.0 = Critical

Other factors can affect how vulnerable a system is that cannot be captured in the CVSS scoring. For example, a CVE with a score of 10 (critical) on a web browser is bad, but what if the system has no connection to the Internet or internal networks and the browser is only used to access an application that is only on that system? This significantly reduces the risk and the impact if the system is compromised.

From the assessor's perspective, they record the network scan data, and it is the responsibility of the system owners and stakeholders to explain why the system has reduced risk.

There are other common scoring methods, such as the Common Weakness Scoring System (CWSS), which is a way to prioritize software weaknesses. CVSS scoring maps large commercially available vendor products and uses confidentiality, integrity, authentication, and availability factors to determine weaknesses.

CWSS is more for software code development and uses base finding, environment, and attack surface to calculate the score.

You will see CWSS in web application scanners, SSL server testing, and penetration testing tools. The weaknesses identified on web applications, other home-grown apps, and firmware are called Common Weakness Enumeration (CWEs). CWEs use CWSS for scoring.

Copyright © 2022 by Bruce Brown

Interpretation and Accuracy

As the assessor, must make sure that the scanner runs successfully. One thing that often happens with credentialed scans is that they don't authenticate successfully on all the target systems. This will not have a great impact if less than 10% of the systems being scanned did not authenticate, but if there are more than that, it can through off the accuracy of the data to the point where the scan needs to be run again.

Another error to look out for is scanning the wrong range of systems. It's important to double-check the scan and have another set of eyes check out the targeted system pool before running the scan.

The reason that it is important to have someone well-versed in the scanner being used is that sometimes there are technical issues that arise with the tool itself. When this happens, the SCA can reach back to the vendor, but there needs to be someone skilled enough on the system to ask the right questions to fix the system.

Red Flags of SC Controls

If the scan shows a lot of critical findings related to end-of-life systems in the DMZ and Internet-facing systems, this is bad. If they are not already hacked, they will be soon. As assessors, we can only report what we see; it's up to them to fix it.

In the documentation, some of the red flags are:

- Lack of network diagram
- Network information that is many years old
- Network documentation does not look like the actual network being assessed
- Public IP addresses on the internal network
- High-value systems publicly accessible

Copyright © 2022 by Bruce Brown

- Networks with sensitive information are not segregated or protected
- No devices, such as a firewall, are between networks with different security postures

Green Flags of Access Management

When an organization has gone the extra mile and gotten a penetration test done, that is a great sign. If they have had a penetration test, they usually do a complete internal and external network scan independently. This means they are very serious about network security.

System and Communications Protections Resources

- NIST SP 800-189, Resilient Interdomain Traffic Exchange
- NIST SP 800-77, Guide to IPsec VPNs
- FIPS 186, Digital Signature Standards (DSS)
- NIST SP 800-63-3, Digital Identity Guidelines
- FIPS 140-3, Security Requirements for Cryptographic Modules
- NIST IR 7788, Security Risk Analysis of Enterprise Networks Using Probabilistic Attack Graphs
- NIST SP 800-41, Guidelines on Firewalls and Firewall Policy
- NIST SP 800-56, Recommendation for Key-Derivation Methods in Key-Establishment Schemes
- NISTIR 7956, Cryptographic Key Management Issues & Challenges in Cloud Services
- NISTIR 7966, Security of Interactive and Automated Access Management Using SSH
- NIST SP 800-57 (Part 1 - 5), Recommendation for Key Management

Copyright © 2022 by Bruce Brown

SI – System and Information Integrity

SI controls deal with system and information integrity. In this control family, the assessor is validating the vulnerability management, antivirus/spam, system monitoring, information input validation, and essentially anything protecting the organization's information from unauthorized manipulation. Some of the top controls that are a cornerstone of the SI family are:

- SI-1, Policy, and Procedures
- SI-2, Flaw Remediation
- SI-3, Malicious Code Protection
- SI-4, System Monitoring
- SI-10, Input Validation (for web applications)

For an assessor, these SI controls will tell a lot about the overall risk to the assessed system. This, of course, depends on many other factors, such as the environment, mitigating controls, and threats to the system.

Examination of SI – System and Information Integrity Controls

The assessor should examine the organization's policy to determine how (or if) they address flaw remediation, malicious code protection, system monitoring, and input validation. These are fancy words for vulnerability management, antivirus, audit log monitoring, and user input web pages.

Flaw Remediation (SI-2)

This control will be mapped to many of the vulnerabilities that pop up in the network scans. Flaw remediation means fixing systems when

Copyright © 2022 by Bruce Brown

errors, updates, or new vulnerabilities are discovered. The artifacts that can be examined are:

- The vulnerability management plan, policy, procedure
- Network scan results
- Remediation plan
- Plan of action and milestone to update software
- Patch management documentation
- Patch management results
- System security plan
- System security policy

There is no system without flaws, but the assessor is looking for the organization to have an effective process of dealing the these weaknesses in a timely manner.

Antimalware, System Monitoring, and SPAM

Antivirus, antimalware, endpoint protection response, and antispam are part of the SI family. The assessor needs to see if the organization has identified a solution for doing malicious code protection (SI-3) and if it has been installed on the target system or implemented on the network to protect the systems being assessed. Virus signatures are what get a lot of organizations. For whatever reason, sometimes they don't update them regularly. Some systems cannot connect to the vendor to automatically update the signatures, so the organization must develop a method of updating the signatures manually or in a central location controlled locally.

Antispam is not always a requirement of the organization or system that is being assessed (SI-8). It might not apply if the system being assessed does not process emails. But if it does, the SCA will see the antispam solution and if it has been installed and enabled on the system in testing.

Copyright © 2022 by Bruce Brown

Antimalware solutions will often be part of a larger system monitoring solution. The assessor will look for a process where the organization monitors audit logs, looking for patterns of behavior that might show an attack or unauthorized activities (SI-4). This might be part of a security operations center, cybersecurity analyst team, or an information and event management system that pulls logs from multiple places. On very small networks or stand-alone systems, the monitoring process might be as simple as an event log review once per quarter. The assessor will be looking for the activity to be documented.

The artifacts that the assessor can check out are:

- System security plan & policy
- Software inventory showing antivirus software
- System baseline showing antivirus software installed
- System scan show when antivirus software is out of date
- Screenshots showing the antimalware software installed
- Incident response records
- Incident response procedures

Examination of Information Input Validation

For systems with frontend interfaces such as web applications or databases collecting user information, the assessor may examine the restrictions on information input.

The system should validate the input of users. For example, users might be forced to only type in letters if a first name is needed in a data input field. There might also be a character limit in input fields that access databases, so attackers cannot exploit a query by typing in complex commands.

The assessor should look for documentation such as standards, plans, and procedures that detail what is allowed. The organization

Copyright © 2022 by Bruce Brown

might also add metadata and messages that tell the user what is expected in the input field. Other things that can be used to observe the uses of information input validation include:

- Configuration settings of the software input box
- Application policy
- Work instructions detailing user input restrictions
- User instructions with user input restrictions
- Source code

Interview for the SI Family

The SI controls that the assessor will focus one will depend on what is being evaluated. SI controls may have many different stakeholders to interview.

Cybersecurity professionals will have a good idea about antivirus and system monitoring. While Spam (or anything dealing with email) usually has its own team, but cybersecurity should know the security features of content filtering in the organization.

System administrators or software engineers will usually do input validation. Remember that these roles vary in every organization, and all interviews must be set up before the assessment starts so that these key personnel are available.

Here are some good questions to get an idea of the SI control status:

- Is there a policy that addresses patching, antivirus, monitoring, or information integrity? (SI-1)
- What is the vulnerability management process for this system? (SI-2)
- How are vulnerabilities identified, reported, and corrected? (SI-2)
- Before being patched or upgraded, how are systems tested? (SI-2)

Copyright © 2022 by Bruce Brown

- Is there any malicious code protection (antivirus) used on the system? (SI-3)

- How are the virus signatures updated for the antivirus software? (SI-3)

- How does the antivirus system work? Is it centralized? (SI-3)

- Is there a method to detect potential attacks on the network? (SI-4)

- How does the organization identify unauthorized uses of systems? (SI-4)

- Are potential security incidents and anomalies analyzed?

Testing for the SI Family

The SCA will need to test the behavior of SI tools, apps, and processes that protect the integrity of content and systems within the assessment's scope. Access to these systems may require subject matter experts with privileged access. These will likely be the same people that are needed for the interview.

The assessor will need to be knowledgeable enough about the tools or applications being tested to recognize what the system is supposed to do, regardless of the vendor.

The tools to test include:

- Antimalware / Antivirus (SI-4, SI-3)

- Endpoint protection systems (SI-4, SI-3)

- Spam filters

- Endpoint detection and response systems (SI-4, SI-3)

- Security information and event management systems (SI-4, SI-3)

- Intrusion detection systems (SI-4, SI-3)

Copyright © 2022 by Bruce Brown

These are just some of the tools that can be tested. On powerful and complex tools, it's best to let the system administrator or cybersecurity professional login and navigate the system. Let the administrator of the system drive while you tell them where you want them to go (like a driver's test).

The assessor should check whether the tools used are up to date and if it matches the organization's needs. Does the solution match the security policy the organization has put in place?

Red Flags of SI Controls

A red flag is when the organization has had security incidents that affected the network from a phishing attack. Malware downloaded from the Internet attempts to exploit flaws in the software. If the organization is not remediating systems inside the network, the assessor is bound to detect a lot of findings.

A lack of vulnerability management is a common issue. In cases like this, you will find:

- Lots of end-of-life systems in mission essential parts of the system
- Overwhelming numbers of vulnerabilities
- No plans to fix the vulnerabilities

Green Flags of SI Controls

When the organization is really on top of its game, they have a robust vulnerability management program that fixes flaws at a rate that matches the severity of the finding.

SI - System and Information Integrity Resource

- NIST SP 800-128, Guide for Security-Focused Configuration Management of Information Systems
- FIPS 186, Digital Signature Standards (DSS)

Copyright © 2022 by Bruce Brown

- ☀ FIPS 140-3, Security Requirements for Cryptographic Modules

- ☀ NIST IR 7788, Security Risk Analysis of Enterprise Networks Using Probabilistic Attack Graphs

- ☀ NIST SP 800-40, Guide to Enterprise Patch Management Technologies

Copyright © 2022 by Bruce Brown

SR – Supply Chain Risk Management

Supply chain risk management (SR controls) are assessed based on the organization's processes to ensure that all materials, tools, and services are from secure sources and not compromised. If the organization is purchasing external hard drives from a vendor, it should ensure the vendor's business, product, and support are stable and approved. The organization should know if the federal, state, and industry have any restrictions on the vendor. The assessor will see this process documented and approved by upper-level management or maybe have a work role dedicated to managing the supply chain risk. Even if there is a role or an entire department, such as acquisitions, dedicated to making sure the products and services used by the organization are secure and approved, supply chain risk management is everyone's job, so if the assessor sees the chief financial officer supplying the office with flash drives bought from Walmart with their funds, bypassing all process and then plugging them into the work systems because its "no big deal," they should put this detail in their risk assessment report.

The most used and visible SR controls include:

- SR-2, Supply Chain Risk Management Plan
- SR-3, Supply Chain Controls and Processes

Examination of SR – Supply Chain Risk Management Controls

No "one size fits all" supply chain risk management (SCRM) programs exist. Each organization has different mission and business needs, so their supply requirements and regulations will differ. If the supply chain is part of the assessment, the assessor needs to observe the organization's SCRM to get an idea of what they say they are supposed to be doing. The assessor should look for policies and a

Copyright © 2022 by Bruce Brown

procedure that is up to date and approved according to the organization own policy or industry standards.

What is in the SCRM depends on what is being supplied and those needs are based on the organization's mission and business needs. As assessors, we cannot tell them what needs to be supplied.

The assessor should focus on whether the organization considers the risks of dealing with a supplier. For example, if the tools or services require a direct network connection, the SCRM policy might mention the importance of the vendor's cybersecurity posture and threats to the supplier. The vendor might need a regular assessment or certification to continue to be a supplier to the organization.

Another example might be that the organization can only purchase software from an approved application list that has already been verified. Counterfeit or products from certain countries might also be a factor.

The assessor's focus is that the organization first has a supply chain process and then addresses the risk of what is being supplied or who is supplying the goods and services. This should be in a process, plan, policy, or other document management approval.

Some of the documents that the assessor can review include:

- System security plan SR implementation statements
- Contract or agreement language mentioning governance, risk, or compliance
- SCRM plan, policy, or procedures
- Acquisition documents with purchasing restrictions or risk management strategies
- Business-to-business network interconnection agreements
- Shipping & Trade policies
- Export controls policy

Copyright © 2022 by Bruce Brown

- Standards that match international regulations on trade

Interviews for SR – Supply Chain Risk Management Controls

Acquisitions, human relations, cybersecurity, management, and compliance professionals will be the people to point you in the right direction for supply chain risk management. This is sometimes its unit within an organization or integrated as a task to compliance, human relations, or acquisitions.

As SCAs, our mission is to find out if the organization has an SCRM process, whether it is documented properly, and how it aligns with the NIST 800 SR controls that are relevant to the organization's system that is being assessed.

The interview allows one to see how much the subject matter experts know about the SCRM and what is being done that aligns with their policy.

- Are the contracts and agreements with outside suppliers up to date?

- Are the agreements with outside services still valid?

- Do contracts and agreements address relevant compliance issues? (For example, retail contracts mention PCI compliance or federal systems require a certain level of vendor support).

- Is compliance mentioned in agreements or contracts?

- Is there a supply chain risk management process?

- Is the supply chain risk management process documented?

- Are there restrictions on what products or services are acquired? (Example, approved software/hardware list, approved vendors list)

- Have hardware and software providers been acquired from approved sources?

Copyright © 2022 by Bruce Brown

- Are maintenance contracts current?

- Is there a policy for international trade and exports of products and services? (If applicable)

Testing for SR – Supply Chain Risk Management Controls

In addition to documents, the organization may have acquisition and contracting tools that help with the supply chain risk (SR-5). The assessor can test these tools to validate how they help the organization manage the risk. These tools could include:

- Tracking the shipping status – If applicable, shipping can be sent to and from secure locations; confidentiality might be a factor.

- Secure and Controlled Order process – Not everyone in the organization can order anything.

- Supplier management systems

- Security rating systems – An example of this might be BitSight which assigns a risk-based score based on vendors' cybersecurity.

- Vendor compliance systems

The assessor will need a subject matter expert to help walk through and explain what each SCRM tool does. This is a great opportunity to integrate questions with testing as the subject matter expert logs in and navigates the system.

The assessor should ask, "does the organization use BitSight to determine the risk of vendors they work with?" "Can you show me the risk score of what of your vendors?" or "How does the organization use the vendor compliance systems?"

BitSight is just an example, and most organizations will not use the tools mentioned here. The point is to prompt the system

Copyright © 2022 by Bruce Brown

administrators as they navigate the system so the assessor can get an idea of whom is being used to manage the risk to the supply chain.

Red Flags of SR Controls

If employees buy mission-critical components from random places with personal funding, this should bring many questions. As the assessor, you should ask if there is a process they should be following and have the employees be made aware of it.

Green Flags of SR Controls

If there are automated methods of tracking and controlling the supply chain, this would be great for medium and large organizations. When acquisitions, IT, and cybersecurity know the supply chain process, the organization has done its job.

SR - Supply Chain Risk Management Resource

- NIST SP 800-161, Supply Chain Risk Management Practices for Federal Information Systems and Organizations
    - nvlpubs.nist.gov
- NIST C-SCRM
    - https://csrc.nist.gov/Projects/cyber-supply-chain-risk-management
- Federal Acquisition Supply Chain Security Act
    - https://www.federalregister.gov
    - https://www.congress.gov/bill/115th-congress/senate-bill/3085
- Executive Order 13873, "Securing the Information and Communications Technology and Services Supply Chain
- https://www.federalregister.gov

Copyright © 2022 by Bruce Brown

Conclusion

The assessment is one of the most important parts of any security framework, from CIS to ISO 27001 to NIST 800. Technology, threats, and vulnerabilities constantly change, so they must be checked, updated, and evaluated. Assessing is a skill that every organization needs. So if you know the techniques, you will be valuable to any organization.

One of the best resources for NIST RMF assessments is the NIST 800-53A, Assessing Security and Privacy Controls in Information Systems and Organizations.

The steps of the process are to prepare by determining the needs of the organization, create a security assessment plan with the "who, what, when, where, and how" of the assessment, conduct the assessment using examination, interviews, and testing and deliver a risk assessment report with all the findings.

The expected results you use to measure the findings are what the organization itself knows it is supposed to be doing, following regulations, directives, and policies.

Copyright © 2022 by Bruce Brown

www.ingramcontent.com/pod-product-compliance
Lightning Source LLC
Chambersburg PA
CBHW021959120726
47992CB00001B/330